Elementary
VOCABULARY
Games

A collection of vocabulary games and activities for elementary students of English

Jill Hadfield

Addison Wesley Longman Limited
Edinburgh Gate, Harlow,
Essex CM20 2JE, England
and Associated Companies throughout the world.

© Jill Hadfield 1998

The right of Jill Hadfield to be identified as author of this Work has been asserted by her in accordance with the Copyright, Designs and Patents Act 1988

Permission to copy

The material in this book is copyright. However, the publisher grants permission for copies of the pages in the sections entitled 'Games material' and 'Rules sheets' to be made without fees as follows: private purchasers may make copies for their own use or for use by classes of which they are in charge; school purchasers may make copies for use within and by the staff and students of the school only. This permission to copy does not extend to additional schools or branches of an institution, who should purchase a separate master copy of the book for their own use.

For copying in any other circumstances prior permission in writing must be obtained from Addison Wesley Longman Ltd.

ISBN 0 582 31270 1

Set by 9/11.5pt Photina MT

Produced through Longman Malaysia

For Laura
who loves words

Acknowledgements

I am very grateful to the staff and students of the EFL section, South Devon College for inspiring and trying out these games, and to Maria Stebbings for her sensitive and skilful editing of the first drafts of this book.

Illustrations by Gary Andrews, Kathy Baxendale, Pete Neame, Pavely Arts, Sue Tewkesbury

Designed by Cathy May (Endangered Species)

Cover photo © Image Bank/MJ Cardenas

Contents

List of topic areas for games	**3**
Introduction	**4**
Teacher's notes	**7**
Games material	**32**
Rules sheets	**118**

List of topic areas for games

1. Family members
2. Countries and nationalities
3. Jobs
4. Colours
5. Parts of the body
6. Faces
7. Clothes
8. Rooms in a house
9. Furniture
10. Household objects
11. Kitchen objects
12. Food and drink
13. Fruit and vegetables
14. Shops
15. Shopping lists
16. Containers
17. Seasons, months, days of the week
18. Weather
19. Everyday actions
20. Work activities
21. Household tasks
22. Hobbies
23. Sports
24. Movements
25. Shapes and patterns
26. Materials
27. Town features
28. Street features
29. Places to live
30. The countryside

Introduction

1 About games

A game is an activity with rules, a goal and an element of fun.

There are two kinds of games: *competitive games*, in which players or teams race to be the first to reach the goal, and *cooperative games*, in which players or teams work together towards a common goal.

The activities in this book fall into two categories: *linguistic games* and *communicative games*. In linguistic games, the goal of the game is linguistic accuracy: producing a correct structure, or, in the case of these vocabulary games, remembering the correct word. Communicative games, however, are activities with a goal or aim that is not linguistic. Successful completion of the game will involve the carrying out of a task such as drawing in a route on a map, filling in a chart, or finding two matching pictures, rather than the correct production of a structure. However, in order to carry out this task it will be necessary to use language and, by careful construction of the task, it will be possible to specify in advance what language will be required.

These games can be used at all stages of the progression from controlled to free practice, serving at one end of the range as a memory aid and repetition drill, at the other, as a chance to use language freely and as a means to an end rather than an end in itself. They can also serve as a diagnostic tool for the teacher, who can note areas of difficulty and take appropriate remedial action.

2 About vocabulary

I started writing this book because I became interested in the process of acquiring vocabulary, i.e. the processes that go on *after* the introduction and explanation of new vocabulary. How do we remember new words? How do we expect our students to remember them? How can a new word or a set of new words become integrated into our existing word store? How can we become so familiar with it that we can locate it and pull it out again when we need to use it?

Remembering new words is hard. Words are very slippery things. Before you know it, they've wriggled away and are gone. It takes a lot of effort to keep them where you want them. It seems to me that in order to retain a word, students have to go through three distinct processes. They have to fix the meaning of the word in their minds, they have to somehow make the word their own – to personalise it so that it takes on a colour and a character for them and becomes part of their individual word store – and they have to use the word creatively in context for themselves.

The question for me, in writing this book, was firstly:

How could I devise activities that would help the learner through these three processes?

- Fix the meaning of the word in your mind.
- Make the word your own.
- Use the word to communicate with others.

And secondly: How could I make it fun?

3 About this book

This book is a resource book of practice activities for vocabulary: the games have been designed to *practise*, not to introduce, new vocabulary. The book assumes that introduction and explanation of the vocabulary has been done in the textbook or other course that the teacher and class is following.

The vocabulary items have been arranged in lexical sets following topics used in most textbooks and courses at this level. The topic area, vocabulary focus, structures and any additional vocabulary (not the main focus) that the students will need are all listed at the beginning of each game. The structures have been kept to an elementary level and are for each game what a student at this stage could reasonably be expected to know.

Each game has three stages: *memorising*, *personalising* and *communicating*, taking the student through the three processes described above, though the three stages are self-contained so that the teacher is free to select or discard any stage, according to what she feels her students need.

The games make use of a variety of techniques. Variety is important in language teaching, and a succession of games based on the same principles, though exciting and novel at first, would soon pall. Techniques used include information gap, guessing, search, matching, exchanging, collecting, combining, arranging, and card games, board games, puzzles and role-play.

The simplest activities are based on the *information gap* principle. In these activities Student A has access to some information which is not held by Student B. Student B must acquire this information to complete a task successfully. This type of game may be *one-sided*, as in the above example, or *reciprocal*, where both players have information which they must pool to solve a common problem. The games may be played in pairs or small groups, where all the members of the group have some information.

Guessing games are a familiar variant on this principle. The player with the information deliberately withholds it, while others guess what it might be.

Search games are another variant, involving the whole class. In these games everyone in the class has one piece of information. Players must obtain all or a large amount of the information available to fill in a questionnaire or to solve a problem. Each student is thus simultaneously a giver and a collector of information.

Matching games are based on a different principle, but also involve a transfer of information. These games involve matching corresponding pairs of cards or pictures, and may be played as a whole class activity, where everyone must circulate until they find a partner with a corresponding card or picture; or a pairwork or small group activity, where players must choose pictures or cards from a selection to match those chosen by their partner from the same selection; or as a card game on the 'snap' principle.

Matching-up games are based on a jigsaw or 'fitting together' principle. Each player in a group has a list of opinions, preferences, wants or possibilities. Through discussion and compromise the group must reach an agreement.

Exchanging games are based on the 'barter' principle. Players have certain articles, cards or ideas which they wish to exchange for others. The aim of the game is to make an exchange which is satisfactory to both sides.

Exchanging and collecting games are an extension of this. Players have certain articles or cards which they are willing to exchange for others in order to complete a set. This may be played as a whole class activity, where players circulate freely, exchanging articles or cards at random; or as an inter-group activity, where players agree to collect a certain set of articles as a group and then exchange articles between groups; or as a card game on the 'rummy' principle.

Combining activities are those in which the players must act on certain information in order to arrange themselves in groups such as families or people spending holidays together.

Arranging games are also sometimes called *sequencing* or *ordering games*. These are games where the players must acquire information and act on it in order to arrange items in a specific order. Items to be arranged can be picture cards, events in a narrative, or even the players themselves!

Board games and *card games* are familiar game types, where the aim is to be the first round a board, or to collect the most cards, or to get rid of the cards first. The cards and squares on the board are used as stimuli to provoke a communication exchange.

All the above activities may include elements of puzzle-solving, role-play, or simulation.

Puzzle-solving activities occur when participants in the game share or pool information in order to solve a puzzle or a mystery: Where did the aliens come from? Did Annie commit the murder? etc.

Many games include an element of *role-play*. Players are given the name and some characteristics of a fictional character. However, these are not role-plays in the true sense, as the role-play element is always subordinate to the game for the purposes of language use. The outcome of a game is 'closed'; once cards are distributed it develops in a certain predetermined way, while role-play proper is open-ended and may develop in any number of ways.

The three games in each unit are all different in nature and make use of different techniques.

The first game in each unit is a *memorisation game*, designed to fix the meaning of the word in the student's mind. These games are linguistic games as distinct from the other two activities in the unit which focus on communication; their focus is on accuracy rather than fluency and for the most part they only require the student to produce single words rather than sentences. The games used in this stage are very simple versions of matching (including lotto and bingo games), sorting, ordering, guessing (including mime games), arranging and collecting. In each case, the aim of the game is to get the students to remember and produce the right word (matching words to pictures for example, or guessing which word is being mimed or sorting words into two lexical sets).

The activities in the second stage (*personalising*) are not really games, but humanistic activities designed to get the students to relate the new words to their personal experience. They fall into two stages: a reflective phase, where students are asked to visualise something or associate the words with their personal life and preferences, and a communicative phase where they are asked to share what they have thought or written with others. The language in this stage is also fairly controlled (sentence patterns and frames are often given), though the students will now need to produce whole utterances not single words.

The activities in the third stage are *communication games* where the focus is on successful completion of a goal such as finding a person, solving a puzzle or completing a drawing, rather than on correct production of lexis and structures. In this stage, language is less controlled and there is more flexibility and creativity required of the students. Games in this section include the whole range of communicative games: matching, searching, information gap, puzzle solving, role-play, arranging and ordering and exchanging and collecting games.

4 Some practical considerations

A] *Classroom management*

There are three main types of activities in this book: *pair work*, involving two partners, *small group work*, involving groups of three or four, and *whole class activities*, where everyone moves freely around the room. All these activities require some flexibility in the constitution of groups and organisation of the classroom. It is best to have the desks in a U-shape if possible. Students can then work with the person sitting next to them for pair work, and groups of threes and fours can easily be constituted by alternate pairs moving their chairs to the inner side of the U, opposite another pair. Whole class activities, which involve all the students circulating freely, can take place in the empty area in the centre of the U-shape. Simulation activities may involve special arrangements of furniture and suggestions are made in the Teacher's notes for these activities. If it is not possible to arrange desks in this way, this need not deter you! The traditional arrangement of front-facing desks can be easily adapted to pair work, with people at adjoining desks working together, while small groups can be formed by two people turning their chairs round to face the people behind them. Whole class activities present a little more of a problem, but often there is a space big enough for the students to move around in at the front of the class, or desks can be pushed back to clear a space in the centre.

Where possible, an alternative small group version of the whole class games in this book has been provided, so that teachers who experience a great deal of difficulty with the kind of games that require students to move around, can play these games in a more static format.

Games are best set up by demonstration rather than by lengthy explanation. The teacher should explain briefly what the game involves, hand out the photocopied cards, giving the students a little time to study them, and then demonstrate the game with one of the students in front of the class. It will be found that the idea of the game is probably easier for students to grasp from seeing the cards than from a verbal explanation, and that, as they become more familiar with the idea of the games and the techniques used, any initial problems caused by unfamiliarity will quickly disappear. Where more complicated card games are played in small groups, it is suggested that teachers hand out a photocopied Rules sheet to each group of students together with the card(s). There is a reference in the Teacher's notes for each game to indicate where Rules sheets are provided. These are to be found at the back of the book, after the games material section.

Some of the games in this book involve role-play. Role-plays involve two distinct phases: preparation and production. In the preparation phase students should be given sufficient time to digest the information on the role card and to ask the teacher for help with anything they do not understand. When the students are sufficiently prepared, and all the problems of comprehension are ironed out, the role-play can begin. Encourage the students not to rely too heavily on looking at their role cards, but to remember the information. With the shorter role cards it is a good idea to collect them in before the role-play begins.

The teacher's role in these activities is that of monitor and resource centre, moving from group to group, listening, supplying any necessary language, noting errors, but not interrupting or correcting as this impedes fluency and spoils the atmosphere. It is a good idea to carry paper and pen and to note any persistent errors or areas of difficulty. These can then be dealt with in a feedback session after the game. In many cases the game could then be played again with different partners or with different role cards.

The average length of time for the games in the book is about 15-20 minutes. All three games in each unit could therefore be played in an average lesson. The games in the Game 3 section of two units (17 and 27) are a little longer or more complicated, taking 30 minutes or so, and these have been indicated with the words 'Long game' in a box at the beginning.

B] Resource management

The resources required for each game fall into two categories: reusable and disposable. Where a very small number of photocopies are needed for a whole class game or where students may write on their cards, it is best to treat these photocopies as disposable. For example, Game 3 in *Unit 2 Countries and nationalities* requires the students to write on the copies. There is no point, therefore, in collecting up the photocopies in order to use them with another class when the game is finished.

In contrast, most of the games in this book require a larger number of copies and an investment of the teacher's time in accurate copying, cutting up etc., so it is worthwhile thinking of these materials as reusable resources. For example, Game 1 in most units requires a set of cards for each pair of students in the class. The students will not need to write anything on the cards, and as these are mostly quiet games with only two people involved, the cards should reach the end of the game in much the same state as they began. It is worth, therefore, investing some time in making the photocopies into a permanent class set of materials. If you have the time and resources, obviously printing or pasting the materials onto card or laminating them would help preserve their shelf-life. If you don't have the time or the resources, however, this isn't absolutely necessary: I have sets of games materials printed only on to paper, that have done their duty in workshops all over the world and aren't much the worse for wear after five years. What is more important is providing a system to prevent the materials getting lost and disorganised. If you have a class set of ten sets of cards, for example, it is worth putting each set into an envelope clearly labelled with the name of the game and the number of cards. It is then the students' responsibility to collect up all the cards at the end of the game, check that they are all there, put them back into the envelope and hand them back to you. If two sets of cards are required for a game, keep them in two smaller envelopes inside the big one, and get the students to sort them back into their respective envelopes at the end of the game.

Two specialised copying techniques are called for in this book. One is colour copying (in *Unit 4*). As the cards in this game are a reusable resource, it might be worthwhile making one coloured set yourself, following the guidance in the *Materials and preparation* section of the game, and then taking it to a colour copier shop to make ten or so copies. These would then last through several generations of students. If you cannot get to a colour copier shop, however, you can still make the materials by getting the students to colour them, following your instructions. The other technique, back-to-back copying, is used in many games in this book, where cards will have a picture on one side and the word on the other. The symbol ↔ is printed at the top of the pages to indicate where back-to-back printing is needed. If your copier will do back-to-back, this should present no problem, though you will have to be fairly careful about aligning the sheets so that the words are printed on the backs of the correct pictures! If you cannot print back-to-back, there are two solutions: (1) make two sets of cards, one with pictures and one with words. This solution means that you will have to adapt the games with the picture/word cards into simpler matching games as in Game 1 in *Unit 12 Food and drink*. This solution obviously restricts the range of games available to you, so it is better in the long run to adopt solution (2): write the words on the backs yourself, or, better still, get the students to do it – this could form part of a vocabulary practice exercise (though you will have to check they've done it correctly!).

Finally, if you have no access to copying facilities at all, it is possible, though time-consuming, to make home-made versions of the materials by getting the students to work with you to draw and write the cards. You would need to give every student a sheet of paper and instruct them how to divide it up into squares. Then either dictate to the students what to draw or write in each square, or make large drawings of the cards on the board for them to copy. Ask the students to cut up the cards when they have finished and put them into an envelope. In this way, you will have a reusable class set of materials.

Teacher's notes

1 Family members

Topic area
family members

Vocabulary focus
aunt, brother, cousin, daughter, father, granddaughter, grandfather, grandmother, grandson, husband, mother, nephew, niece, sister, son, uncle, wife

Extra vocabulary
numbers

Structures
be, *have*, possessive *'s*

Materials and preparation

GAME 1 Copy the picture cards, family tree 1 and relationship cards. (Remember to copy the relationship cards on both sides.) You will need one set for each pair. Cut up the picture cards and relationship cards.

GAME 2 No materials.

GAME 3 Copy and cut up family tree 2 (set of four cards). You will need one set for every group of three or four in your class.

How to use the games

GAME 1 Memorising
pairwork puzzle

- Divide the students into pairs.
- Give one set of picture cards, relationship cards and family tree 1 to each pair.
- They should put the family tree and the picture cards face up on the table, so that they can see them.
- They should place the relationship cards in a pile with the sentences face up.
- They should take it in turns to take a relationship card from the pile and read it out. They should then try to put the picture cards in the right places on the family tree according to the information on the card. (This will get easier as they turn up more cards.)
- **The object of the game is to complete the family tree according to the information on the cards.**
- When they have finished and the tree is complete, they should turn over the relationship cards so the reverse side is visible.
- They should then take it in turns to take a card and make a statement about the two or three people mentioned. They can check they are right by turning over the card. If they are right, they can keep the card. The player with the most at the end is the winner.

GAME 2 Personalising
small group discussion

- Put students in groups of three or four.
- Ask them to complete the following group totals:

  In our group we have (x) brothers.
  sisters.
  sons.
  daughters.
  cousins.
  nephews.
  nieces.
  aunts.
  uncles.

  Alter or amend the list to suit the students in your class.
- **The object of the activity is for each group to calculate how many brothers, sisters etc. they have in the group as a whole.**
- Collect up totals from each group when they have finished.

GAME 3 Communicating
small group information gap game

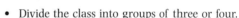

Family jigsaw

- Divide the class into groups of three or four.
- Make one set of family tree 2 cards for each group.
- Each student should take one card. They should not show it to the others.
- They should take it in turns to offer statements about the family from the information on their card.
- When they hear some new information, they should fill in the names on their tree.
- **The object of the game is to share information so that everyone can complete the family tree.**
- When they have all finished, they can compare trees to see if they have arrived at the right result.
- The group to finish first is the winner.

2 Countries and nationalities

Topic area
countries and nationalities

Vocabulary focus
America, American; Australia, Australian; China, Chinese; England, English; France, French; Greece, Greek; Holland, Dutch; India, Indian; Italy, Italian; Mexico, Mexican; Russia, Russian; Spain, Spanish (if you want to teach other countries, you can make additional cards on the models given)

Structures
He's/She's/I'm ... What's your name? Where are you from? I'm from ...
plus: *I've been to ..., I want to go to ...* (for recognition only; can be explained at the time)

Materials and preparation

GAME 1 Copy and cut up the country cards and the people cards. Don't forget to copy the country cards on both sides. You will need one set for each pair of students.

GAME 2 No materials. (You might like to write up

I'VE BEEN TO   I WANT TO GO TO

as two column headings on the board.)

GAME 3 Copy the country cards sheet (picture side only), but do not cut it up. Make one copy for every student. Copy enough people cards for every student to have one each (of the appropriate sex if possible).

NOTE: If you don't want your class to learn all the countries and nationalities on the cards, simply select those you feel appropriate. If you want additional countries and nationalities, make extra cards yourself on the same model.

How to use the games

GAME 1   Memorising

pairwork matching

1

- Divide the class into pairs.
- Give each pair a set of (cut up) country cards and a set of (cut up) people cards.
- They should use the country cards first.
- They should spread the cards out, picture-side up, so that they can see all of them.
- They should then take turns to pick a card up and name the country. They can check their answer by looking on the back. If they are right, they can keep the card, if not, they must put it back.
- **The object of this part of the game is to collect cards by naming the countries correctly.**
- The player who has collected most cards at the end is the winner.

2

- Then the country cards should be spread out again, and the people cards should be placed in a pile face down.
- They should take it in turns to turn up a card from the people pile and match it with the corresponding country card, saying 'He's Australian' or 'She's Italian' etc.
- They can check by turning the country card over and reading the back. If they are right, they can keep the card. If not, they should put it at the bottom of the pile.
- **The object of this part of the game is to collect cards by naming the nationality correctly.**
- The player with most cards at the end is the winner.

GAME 2   Personalising

pairwork discussion

- Put up headings for two lists on the board:
  I'VE BEEN TO   I WANT TO GO TO
  Explain briefly what these mean.
- Ask the students to write lists of countries under these two headings.
- When they have finished, join them up with a partner and ask them to tell each other about their lists.

GAME 3   Communicating

whole class search game

Missing persons

- Give every student in the class a copy of the page of country cards (not cut up) and one of the people cards.
- Ask them to imagine they are the person on the card they have been given. They should write their name on the country sheet by the country they come from.
- **The object of the game is to find out who everyone in the class is, and where they are from, and to fill in the country sheet with the names.**
- To do this, students will need to move around the class, asking 'What's your name?' and 'Where are you from?' and filling in names in the appropriate countries.

3 Jobs

Topic area
jobs

Vocabulary focus
architect, artist, builder, bus driver, businessman, car mechanic, chef, dentist, doctor, engineer, factory worker, farmer, firefighter, hairdresser, journalist, nurse, pilot, police officer, postman, scientist, secretary, shop assistant, student, teacher (or a selection from these as appropriate for your class)

Extra vocabulary
family members

Structures
be, What's your job?/What do you do? What's your name? I'm/He's/She's a ...

Materials and preparation

GAME 1 Copy and cut up the picture cards. Remember to copy on both sides. You will need one set for each pair of students in your class.

GAME 2 No materials.

GAME 3 From the picture card sheets, choose as many jobs as there are students in your class (e.g. if you have twelve students, choose twelve jobs). Make five copies of these twelve jobs. (You do not need to copy the words on the reverse side this time.) Cut the first sheet up into individual job cards – one for each student in the class. Cut the remaining four copies up into (vertical) strips of four jobs so that each student will have a strip of four job pictures. (The aim is for each student to have one individual job card plus a strip of four pictures.)

NOTE: If you don't feel your class need to learn all the jobs, simply select those you feel appropriate for the class. For Game 3, if you have taught fewer jobs in Game 1 than the number of students in your class, just play the game in two groups.

How to use the games

GAME 1   Memorising
pairwork sorting and matching game

- Divide the students into pairs.
- Give each pair of students a set of job pictures with the names of jobs on the back.
- They should spread the cards out on the table with the pictures uppermost.
- They should take it in turns to pick up a picture card and try to remember the name of the job. They can check if they are right by turning the card over. If they are right, they can keep the card, if not, they should replace it.
- **The object of the game is to collect as many cards as possible.**
- When they have finished, they can spread the cards out with the names uppermost, and work together to divide them into two groups: people who work inside and people who work outside. Again, they can check by looking at the pictures on the back.
- Students can also sort cards in the same way into 'people who wear uniforms' and 'people who don't wear uniforms'.

GAME 2   Personalising
small group discussion

- Put up the following sentence frame:

  My   father   is a/an ... .
       mother
       sister
       brother
       husband
       wife
       aunt
       uncle
       son
       daughter

  Choose the family members to suit the ages of the students in your class.

- Ask the students to write down as many jobs in their family as they can think of in five minutes.
- Then divide the class into small groups as evenly as possible and ask them to share their information.
- Finally, ask them to total up the number of jobs in their group families and to give you a group total. Which group has the largest number of jobs?

GAME 3   Communicating
whole class search game

Jobsearch

- Give every student in the class a job picture card. Tell them to imagine this is their job.
- Then give everyone a strip of four job pictures. Tell them that these are jobs done by people in the class.
- **The object of the game is to find out which students do the jobs in the four pictures.**
- To do this, they will have to stand up and move around the class asking everyone 'What do you do?' until they find the four people who have the jobs in the strip of pictures they have been given.
- Finally, ask the students to get into groups of three or four and share their information. Have they got enough information to match a job with every student in the class? Which group can match the most names with jobs?

4   Colours

Topic area
colours

Vocabulary focus
black, blue, brown, green, grey, mauve, orange, pink, purple, red, white, yellow

Extra vocabulary
bathroom, bedroom, clothes, dining room, favourite, hall, kitchen, living room, paint, room, tin (of paint)

Structures
be, have got, like, want to

Materials and preparation

GAME 1   *Either* colour in one set of the 24 paint tin cards yourself, following the colours listed in *Vocabulary focus* (each colour should appear twice) and use a colour copier to make ten or more sets. You will need one set per group of 3-4 students in your class. *Or* you can get the students to colour in the paint tins, according to your instructions.

GAME 2   No materials.

GAME 3   Mentally divide the number of students in your class by four. Make that number of copies of the paint tins sheet and cut them up.

NOTE: If you don't want your students to practise all the words, simply select the ones you feel they need.

How to use the games

GAME 1   Memorising
small group 'Snap' game

- Divide the students into groups of three or four.
- Give each group a set of 24 paint cards.
- They should deal out all the cards. Each player should keep his cards in a pile face down in front of him.
- The game is played like 'Snap': each player in turn takes the top card from his pile and places it face up in the middle. When two cards the same follow one another, the first player to shout the name of the colour can collect up the pile of cards and add them to their own pile.

- **The object of the game is to collect all the cards.**
- The game is finished when one player has all the cards.

GAME 2 Personalising
pairwork discussion

- Give the students the following sentence frames to complete:

  My favourite colours are ... .
  I don't like ... .
  A lot of my clothes are ... .
  My room at home is ... .

- When they have finished, put them in pairs to share information.

GAME 3 Communicating
whole class search game

Interior design

- Ask the students to imagine they are redecorating their houses and give them the following sentence frames to complete:

  I want to paint my   dining room   ... .
                           kitchen
                           bathroom
                           bedroom
                           living room
                           hall

  They should complete the sentences with the names of six different colours.

- Then divide the class in half. Get one half to remain seated at their desks and distribute the paint cards evenly among them. They are the paint shops.
- The other half should stand up. They are the customers and should go to the shops to look for the paint they need.
- **The object of the game is for each customer to obtain the six tins of paint she needs to paint her house.**
- To do this, students will have to go from shop to shop asking for the paint they need, until they have all six tins. (There may be a run on certain colours, so some customers may remain unsatisfied!)
- When the game is over, the students can swap roles so that the customers become the shopkeepers and vice versa.

5 Parts of the body

Topic area
parts of the body

Vocabulary focus
arm, back, chest, elbow, finger, foot, hand, head, leg, neck, shoulder, stomach, toe

Extra vocabulary
big, long, round, short, small, square; lift, rub, touch, waggle

Structures
have got, imperatives

Materials and preparation

GAME 1 Copy and cut up the body picture cards and body outline. You will need one body outline and one set of body picture cards for each pair. Don't forget to copy the reverse side too.

GAME 2 No materials.

GAME 3 Mentally divide your class into small groups of three or four. Copy and cut up two sets of robot cards for each group. There is a Rules sheet for this game at the back of the book. Make one copy per group.

NOTE: If you don't want your students to practise all the words, simply select the cards you feel are appropriate.

How to use the games

GAME 1 Memorising
pairwork arranging game

- Divide the students into pairs.
- Give each pair one set of body picture cards and a body outline.
- Ask them to spread the cards out on the desk with the word side uppermost.
- They should take it in turns to take a word card and place it in the appropriate place on the body outline.
- **The object of the game is to build up a body with all the parts in the right places.**
- At the end, they can check if they were right by turning the cards over to see the pictures: they should make a body outline with all the bits in the right places.

GAME 2 Personalising
small group mime game

- Teach the words *rub, waggle, lift, touch* by demonstration and give a few commands for the students to follow, e.g. 'Touch your eye', 'Lift your hands', 'Rub your nose', 'Waggle your ears' etc. Then do this as a build-up sequence with the students:
  A: Touch your eye.
  B: Touch your eye and lift your hand.
  C: Touch your eye, lift your hand and rub your stomach.

  Finally, give a long command, e.g. 'Touch your eye, rub your stomach, waggle your head and lift your right foot' and see if the students can follow the instruction.

- Put the students in pairs and ask them to make up a long command like the ones above (it should be do-able!). Put a sentence frame on the board for them if they need help.
- Join each pair up with another pair to see if they can carry out each others' commands.

GAME 3 Communicating
small group matching game

The robot game

- Divide the students into groups of three or four.
- Pre-teach *big, long, round, short, small, square* if they do not know the words.
- Give each group two sets of the robot cards.
- Ask them to shuffle the packs together and deal out the cards: four per player. The rest should be placed face down in the middle of the table.
- **The object of the game is to find as many matching pairs as possible.**
- To do this, they should first look at their cards and discard any matching pairs. Then Player 1 should begin by asking any other player if they have a card that matches one of the robots in his hand. He should not show the card, but describe it, e.g. 'Have you got a robot with a big round head, a square body, short arms and long legs?'
- If the other player has the card, he must give it to Player 1, who can match it up and discard the pair. If he does not have the card, Player 1 must take the top card from the pile and add it to his hand. Then it is the next player's turn and so on.
- At the end the winner is the player with most matching pairs.

6 Faces

Topic area
facial features, adjectives for physical description

Vocabulary focus
features: *beard, cheeks, chin, ears, eyebrows, eyelashes, eyes, forehead, hair, lips, moustache, mouth, nose, teeth*

adjectives: *black, blonde, blue, brown, green, red; big, curly, long, pointed, round, short, small, square, straight, thin*

Structures
have got, be

Materials and preparàtion

GAME 1 Copy and cut up the body picture cards from *Unit 5 Parts of the body* and the facial feature cards from this game. Remember to copy on both sides. You will need one set per pair. You will also need to copy and cut up one set of word collocation cards per pair.

GAME 2 No materials.

GAME 3 Mentally divide the number of students in your class by two. Copy that number of faces from the funny faces sheet. Cut each one in half vertically. (If you particularly want to practise colours in this game you will have to colour in the eyes and hair before cutting the cards.)

NOTE: If you don't feel your students need to learn all the words, simply select the cards you feel most appropriate for them in Game 1.

Game 3 requires the words *hair, eyes, nose, mouth, ears, face, beard, moustache* + *black, blonde, short, long, big, small, round, square*, so these should form part of your selection in Game 1 if you intend to follow it with Game 3.

How to use the games
GAME 1 Memorising
pairwork sorting and matching games

1
- Divide your class into pairs.
- Give each pair a set of body picture cards and a set of facial features cards.
- Ask them to mix them up and spread them on the table word-side up.
- **The object of this part of the game is to sort the words into two piles: *face* and *body*.**
- They can check they are right by turning the cards over to see the pictures.

2
- Now give each pair a set of the word collocation cards.
- Ask them to spread them on the table: adjectives down one side and nouns on the other.
- **The object of this part of the game is to make as many correct pairs as possible (e.g. *round eyes* or *small eyes* are possible but not *curly eyes* or *pointed eyes*).**
- Check with the whole class when they have finished.

GAME 2 Personalising
pairwork visualisation

- Ask students to close their eyes and visualise the face of someone they know, a friend, or someone in their family.
- Put them in pairs and ask them to describe their face to their partner.

GAME 3 Communicating
whole class matching game

Funny faces

- Give out the half face cards – one to each student.
- **The object of the game is for each student to find the other half of the face she has been given.**
- To do this, everyone will have to move around the class describing their face to the others until they find someone whom they think has the other half. They can then compare faces to see if they match up.
- When they have found their other half, they should sit down.

7 Clothes

Topic area
clothes

Vocabulary focus
anorak, blouse, bra, coat, dress, dressing gown, gloves, jacket, jeans, jumper, leggings, pants, pyjamas, scarf, shirt, shoes, shorts, skirt, slippers, socks, suit, swimsuit, tie, tights, tracksuit, trainers, trousers, T-shirt, vest, woolly hat

Extra vocabulary
find, favourite, wear

Structures
be, have got, like + -ing (I like/don't like wearing ...), can't (I can't find my ...)

Materials and preparation

GAME 1 Copy the body outline from *Unit 5 Parts of the body* and the clothes cards from here. Don't forget to copy the clothes cards on both sides. You will need one body outline and one set of clothes cards per pair.

GAME 2 No materials.

GAME 3 Copy and cut up the washing lines and rows 1–4 of the clothes cards. (You don't need the words on the back this time.) You will need one washing line card and its corresponding row of clothes for each student in the class.

NOTE: If you don't feel your students need to learn all the words, simply select the cards you feel most appropriate for their level/culture.

To limit the vocabulary in Game 3, either use fewer washing lines, or make one photocopy as a master and tippex out the items of clothes you do not want to practise, before following the instructions above.

How to use the games

GAME 1 Memorising
pairwork sorting and matching games

- Divide the students into pairs.
- Give each pair a body outline and a set of clothes cards.
- Ask them to turn the clothes cards word-side up and spread them out on the table.
- They should take it in turns to place them on the body outline in the appropriate place (e.g. *hat* on the head, *socks* on the feet etc.).
- **The object of the game is to place all the cards in the correct places.**
- When they have finished, they can turn the cards over to see the pictures and check if they were right.
- When all the cards are picture-side up, they can see if they can remember the names of the clothes.

GAME 2 Personalising
pairwork discussion

- Write up the following sentence frames:
   I like wearing ... .
   I don't like wearing ... .
   My favourite clothes are ... .
- Ask the students to complete the sentences for themselves.
- Then put the students in pairs to compare their preferences.

GAME 3 Communicating
whole class search game

The washing line game

- Give each student a washing line card and five clothes cards taken from rows 1-4 of the clothes card page. The clothes cards you give each student should not correspond to the items on their washing line.
- Tell the students that it's a very windy day. The washing has blown off their washing line into someone else's garden. The wind has also blown someone else's washing into their garden.
- **The object of the game is for each student to recover their lost washing.**
- To do this, they will have to get up and move around the class asking if anyone has their lost clothes: e.g. 'I can't find my skirt. Have you got it?'

NOTE: This game can also be played in groups of four. Give each player a different washing line card and deal out the clothes cards. Each player must then find the items of clothing on the washing line, by asking the other players. The first player to find all the items is the winner.

8 Rooms in a house

Topic area
parts of a house

Vocabulary focus
rooms: *attic, bathroom, bedroom, cellar, dining room, garage, garden, hall, kitchen, landing, living room, stairs, study, toilet*

floors: *basement, first floor, ground floor, second floor*

Structures
be, next to, on, This is ...

Materials and preparation

GAME 1 Copy and cut up the room cards. If you do this game in teams, you will need two copies; if you do it in small groups, you will need one copy per group.

GAME 2 No materials.

GAME 3 Copy and cut up the house plans. You will need one copy for each pair.

NOTE: If you don't feel your students need to learn all the words, simply select the cards you feel most appropriate for their level/culture. Game 3 does use all the vocabulary listed, but if there are words you feel your students don't need to remember and produce, just write them in on both plans.

How to use the games

GAME 1 Memorising
team/small group guessing game

- You can play this game in two teams or in small groups of three or four.
- If you play in teams, divide the class into two teams.
- Place one pile of room cards face down at one side of the room and the other on the other side of the room.
- Get two volunteers to come to the front.
- Take the top card off each pile and give it to them.
- They should go back to their teams and mime an action that takes place in that room (e.g. cooking for kitchen, sleeping for bedroom etc.).
- When the team guesses correctly, another person should come up and take the next card off the pile, go back and mime that room and so on.
- **The object of the game is for the team to guess all the rooms correctly.**
- The first team to do so is the winner.

NOTE: If you play in small groups, give each group a pile of cards to place face down in the middle of the table. The members of the group take it in turns to take a card and mime the room. The person who guesses gets the next card.

GAME 2 Personalising
pairwork discussion

Ask students to draw a plan of their own house or flat and to show it to their partner, explaining, 'This is the ...'.

GAME 3 Communicating
pairwork information gap

The geography of the house

- Divide the students into pairs.
- Give one student in each pair house plan A and the other house plan B. They should not show each other their plans.
- **The object of the game is for each student to find out the names of the missing rooms and write them in on the plan.**
- To do this, they will have to tell each other about the rooms in their house plan: 'The ... is next to the ...', 'The ... is on the ground floor' etc.

9 Furniture

Topic area
furniture

Vocabulary focus
kitchen: *cooker, cupboard, fridge, sink, washing machine*
living room: *armchair, bookcase, coffee table, desk, sofa*
dining room: *chairs, lamp, rug, sideboard, table*
bedroom: *bed, chest of drawers, dressing table, mirror, wardrobe*
bathroom: *bath, bathroom cabinet, shower, toilet, washbasin*

Structures
be, have got, need, would like

Materials and preparation

GAME 1   Copy and cut up the flat plan and the furniture cards. Remember to copy the furniture cards on both sides. You will need one plan and one set of cards per pair.

GAME 2   No materials.

GAME 3   Copy and cut up the room plans and the furniture cards. (You don't need the words on the backs this time.) You will need one room plan and its corresponding row of furniture cards for each student in the class.

NOTE: If you don't feel your students need to learn all the words, simply select the cards you feel most appropriate for their level/culture. To reduce the vocabulary load for Game 3, make a copy of the room plans. Tippex out the outlines of the furniture you don't want. (For the game to be fair, there should be an equal number of items in each room!) Then use this as your master. Select the furniture cards to correspond with your master of the room plans.

How to use the games

GAME 1 Memorising
pairwork arranging game

- Divide the students into pairs.
- Give each pair a flat plan and a set of furniture cards.
- Get them to spread the furniture cards out word-side up on the table.
- They should take it in turns to take a furniture card and decide which room it should go into on the flat plan.
- **The object of the game is to put all the furniture into suitable rooms.**
- They can check by looking at the pictures on the back of the cards.
- When they have finished and all the cards are picture-side up, they can see if they can remember all the names.

GAME 2 Personalising
pairwork discussion

- Tell the students they have a house with only one room, where they must cook, eat, live and sleep. They can choose five pieces of furniture to have in this room.

- Ask them to decide on the furniture and draw a plan of their room.
- Then put them in pairs to show each other their plans and explain their choice.

GAME 3 Communicating
whole class/small group search game

Removal men

- Give each student a room plan and five furniture cards. The furniture cards should not correspond to the furniture in their room plan.
- Tell students they have just moved into a new house. Unfortunately the removal men have moved in all the furniture – into the wrong rooms!
- **The object of the game is for each student to get the right furniture for their room.**
- To do this, they will have to get up and move around the class asking if anyone has the furniture they need.

NOTE: This game can also be played in small groups. Give each player in the group a different room plan and deal out the furniture cards. Each player must find the furniture they need by asking the other players if they have it. The first player to get all the furniture he needs is the winner.

10 Household objects

Topic area
common household objects

Vocabulary focus
bedroom: *alarm clock, blanket, duvet, hairdryer, pillow, sheet*

bathroom: *bathmat, facecloth, razor, scales, toothbrush, towel*

kitchen: *clock, pedal bin, radio, tablecloth, tablemats, tray*

living room: *cushion, hi-fi system, picture, TV, vase, video*

Structures
be, have got, need

Materials and preparation

GAME 1 Copy and cut up the house plan and the household object cards. Remember to copy the household object cards on both sides. You will need one house plan and a set of household object cards per pair of students.

GAME 2 One set of household object cards per pair of students.

GAME 3 Copy and cut up the room plans and the household object picture cards. (You don't need the words on the back this time.) You will need one room plan and its corresponding row of household object cards for each student in the class.

NOTE: If you don't feel your students need to learn all the words, simply select the cards you feel most appropriate for their level/culture. To reduce the vocabulary load for Game 3, make a copy of the room plans. Tippex out the objects you don't want. (To make the game fair, there should be the same number of items in each room.) Use this copy as your master and select the household object cards to correspond.

How to use the games
GAME 1 Memorising
pairwork arranging game

- Divide the students into pairs.
- Give each pair a house plan and a set of household object cards.
- Get them to spread the object cards out word-side up on the table.
- They should take it in turns to take a household object card and decide which room it should go into on the house plan.
- **The object of the game is to put all the objects into suitable rooms.**
- They can check by looking at the pictures on the back of the cards.
- When they have finished and all the cards are picture-side up, they can see if they can remember all the names.

GAME 2 Personalising
pairwork discussion

- Get the students to work in pairs.
- Give each a set of household object cards.
- Ask them to spread them out picture-side up.
- They should each write a list of the objects under three headings:
  I'VE GOT   I NEED   I DON'T NEED
- When they have finished, they should compare lists.

GAME 3 Communicating
whole class/small group search game

What a mess!

- Give each student a room card and six household object cards. The household object cards should not correspond to the objects in their room card.
- Tell the students they live in a terribly untidy house. Everything is all over the place. Ask them to try to find the objects that should be in their room.
- **The object of the game is for each student to get the right objects for their room.**
- To do this, they will have to get up and move around the class asking if anyone has the object they need.

NOTE: This game can also be played in small groups. Give each player in the group a different room card and deal out the object cards. Each player must find the objects they need by asking the other players if they have them. The first player to get all the objects he needs is the winner.

11 Kitchen objects

Topic area
common kitchen objects

Vocabulary focus
laying the table: *bowl, fork, glass, knife, plate, spoon*

making tea and coffee: *coffeemaker, cup, jug, kettle, saucer, teapot*

washing and ironing: *clothes horse, clothes pegs, iron, ironing board, laundry basket, soap powder*

washing up: *dishcloth, frying pan, plate rack, saucepan, teatowel, washing-up bowl*

cleaning and hoovering floors: *broom, bucket, dustpan and brush, hoover, mop, scrubbing brush*

Extra vocabulary
lay the table, make tea/coffee, do the washing and ironing, wash up, clean the floors, hoover the floors

Structures
be, have got, keep, need

Materials and preparation

GAME 1 Copy and cut up the kitchen objects cards. Remember to copy the cards on both sides. You will need one set of kitchen object cards per pair of students.

GAME 2 One set of kitchen object cards per pair of students.

GAME 3 Copy and cut up the housework game cards and the kitchen object cards. (You don't need the words on the back this time.) You will need one set of housework game cards and one set of kitchen object cards for each group of 4-5 students in the class. There is a Rules sheet for this game at the back of the book. Make one copy per group.

NOTE: If you don't feel your students need to learn all the words, simply select the cards you feel most appropriate for their level/culture. To reduce the vocabulary load for Game 3, either use fewer tasks, or ask the students to collect fewer objects for each task (four, say, instead of six).

How to use the games

GAME 1 Memorising
pairwork sorting game

- Divide the students into pairs.
- Give each pair a set of object cards.
- Get them to spread them out word-side up.
- Ask them to decide whether each object is used for cooking and eating or cleaning.
- **The object of the game is to sort the cards into two piles:** *cooking and eating* **and** *washing and cleaning*.
- When they have done this, they can check by turning the cards over to see the pictures.
- They can then see if they can remember the word for each picture.

GAME 2 Personalising
pairwork visualisation

- Ask students to look at the kitchen object cards and to try to remember where each thing is kept in their own kitchens.
- They can draw a rough plan and explain to their partner: 'We keep the knives and forks in this drawer here, and the plates are in that cupboard over there' etc.

GAME 3 Communicating
small group collecting game

The housework game

- Divide the students into small groups of four or five.
- Give each group a set of housework game cards and a set of kitchen object cards.
- They should take one housework game card each and deal out four kitchen object cards to each player. The rest should be placed face down in a pile in the middle.
- Ask them to decide which six objects they will need to carry out their task. (If they get stuck, you could put a list of all the objects on the board for them to select from.)
- **The object of the game is for each player to obtain the six kitchen object cards he needs to carry out his task.**
- To do this, Player 1 begins by asking any other player if they have one of the objects she needs, e.g.: 'I need the teapot. Have you got it?'
- If the player has the item, she should give it to Player 1, if not, Player 1 should take a card from the pile. Then it is the next player's turn.
- The first player to get all the necessary items for the task is the winner. (You can check they have the right objects – each row of six pictures in the kitchen object cards corresponds to a task in the housework game cards.)

12 Food and drink

Topic area
food and drink

Vocabulary focus
drink: *beer, coffee, milk, orange juice, soup, tea, wine*

food: *bacon, beef, biscuits, bread, butter, cake, cheese, chicken, cooking oil, eggs, fish, flour, ham, ice cream, jam, lamb, pork, rice, spaghetti, sugar*

Structures
be, have got, would like

Materials and preparation

GAME 1 Copy the food pictures and the word cards separately. You will need one set of picture cards and one set of word cards per pair of students.

GAME 2 One set of food picture cards per pair of students.

GAME 3 Mentally divide your class in half. You will need five food picture cards and five word cards each for this number of students (e.g. for a class of 20 you will need 10 x 5 word cards and 10 x 5 food picture cards). Copy and cut up the picture cards and the word cards, making sure that for each picture you copy a corresponding word card.

NOTE: If you don't feel your students need to learn all the words, simply select the cards you feel most appropriate for their level/culture. Beef, ham, pork, bacon, beer, wine are sensitive items in some cultures. You may have some staple food items (e.g. yams, pitta bread, sherbert) which are unique to the country or culture you are teaching in. You can easily add these in by making a picture card and a word card for each item and then copying as in the instructions.

How to use the games

GAME 1   Memorising
pairwork matching game

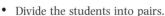

- Divide the students into pairs.
- Give each pair a set of word cards and a set of food picture cards.
- Ask them to spread the picture cards out on the table and to put the word cards face down in a pile.
- They should take it in turns to take the top card from the pile and turn it up.
- **The object of the game is to match words and pictures.**
- The first one to find the matching picture can keep the two cards.
- The player with most cards at the end is the winner.

GAME 2   Personalising
pairwork discussion

- Students should spread the food picture cards out on the table and look at them.
- They should decide on a meal they would like to have and write down all the ingredients.
- Then they should work with a partner and discuss what they have chosen to eat.

GAME 3   Communicating
whole class search game

The high street

- Divide the class in half.
- Give the students in one half five word cards each. They are the shoppers.
- Give the students in the other half five food picture cards each. They are the shopkeepers.
- The shopkeepers should remain at their desks, while the shoppers stand up and move around.
- **The object of the game is for the shoppers to try and find the items on their 'lists'.**
- To do this, they will have to go from 'shop' to 'shop', asking for their items. If a 'shopkeeper' has a picture of one of the items, he should give it to the shopper.
- When the shoppers have found their items, they should sit down.

13 Fruit and vegetables

Topic area
fruit and vegetables

Vocabulary focus
fruit: *apples, bananas, cherries, grapes, lemons, mangoes, melons, oranges, peaches, pears, pineapples, plums, strawberries*

vegetables: *aubergines, avocados, beans, cabbages, carrots, cauliflowers, cucumbers, leeks, lettuces, mushrooms, onions, peas, peppers, potatoes, tomatoes*

Structures
be, have got, like/don't like, some/any

Materials and preparation

GAME 1 Copy the fruit and vegetable cards. Don't forget to copy the words on the back. You will need one set per pair of students.

GAME 2 One set of fruit and vegetable cards per pair of students.

GAME 3 Copy and cut up one set of fruit and vegetables cards for each group of 3-4 students. You don't need the words on the back. There is a Rules sheet for this game at the back of the book. Make one copy per group.

NOTE: If you don't feel your students need to learn all the words, simply select the cards you feel most appropriate for their level/culture. You may have some staple food items (e.g. maize, cassava, beansprouts) which are unique to the country or culture you are teaching in. You can easily add these in by making a picture card and a word card for each item and then copying as in the instructions.

How to use the games

GAME 1   Memorising
pairwork sorting game

- Divide the students into pairs.
- Give each pair a set of fruit and vegetable cards with words on the back.
- Ask them to spread the cards out, word-side up.
- They should divide the cards into two piles: *fruit* and *vegetables*.
- **The object of the first part of the game is to divide the cards up correctly.**
- They can check their decision by looking at the pictures on the back.
- When they have finished checking and all the cards are picture-side up, they can see if they can remember the

word. If they remember correctly, they can keep the card.
- **The object of the second part of the game is to get the most cards.**

GAME 2 Personalising
pairwork discussion
- Divide the students into pairs and give each pair a set of fruit and vegetable cards.
- They should put the cards in a pile picture-side up and take them one at a time from the pile, telling their partner:
  I like ... .
  I don't like ... .

GAME 3 Communicating
small group collecting game
Fruit salad
- Divide the students into groups of three or four and give each group a set of fruit and vegetables cards.
- Ask them to deal out five cards to each player and to put the rest face down in a pile in the middle of the table.
- The players may look at their cards and sort them into fruit and vegetables.
- **The object of the game is to collect a hand of five cards that are either all fruit or all vegetables.**
- Player 1 begins by asking any other player if they have a card that he needs (e.g. 'Have you got any cherries?', if he is collecting fruit).
- If the player he asks has the card, she must give it to him. He takes it, adds it to his hand and throws away a card that he does not want by putting it at the bottom of the pile.
- If she does not have the card, Player 1 must take a card from the pile. If it is a card he wants, he may keep it and throw away another card. If it is not a card he wants, he can throw it away.
- Then it is the next player's turn and so on.
- The winner is the player who is the first to have a hand of all fruit or all vegetables.

14 Shops

Topic area
shops and products

Vocabulary focus
baker's, bookshop, boutique, butcher's, chemist's, department store, DIY store, electrical shop, fishmonger's, florist's, greengrocer's, hairdresser's, jeweller's, newsagent's, shoe shop, sports shop, stationer's, supermarket, sweetshop, toyshop

Extra vocabulary
alarm clock, apples, aspirin, bread, bunch of flowers, butter, chocolates, cookbook, doll, envelopes, fish, haircut, hairdryer, nails, new dress, new shoes, newspaper, steak, suitcase, tennis racket

Structures
be, have got, There is/are ..., Where's ...?; place prepositions (*next to, between, opposite*)

Materials and preparation
GAME 1 Copy the shop cards. Don't forget to copy the products on the back. You will need one set per pair of students.

GAME 2 No materials.

GAME 3 Copy and cut up one set of maps for each group of 3-4 students.

NOTE: If you don't feel your students need to learn all the words, simply select the cards you feel most appropriate for their level/culture. To reduce the vocabulary load for Game 3, make one copy of the maps. If there are words you don't want them to practise, a) ensure that these are written in on every map and b) delete the corresponding item from the shopping list (e.g. if you don't want to practise *DIY store*, write this in on every map, and delete *nails* from the shopping list). Then use this as your copy master.

How to use the games
GAME 1 Memorising
pairwork matching game
- Divide the students into pairs.
- Give each pair a set of shop cards.
- Ask them to put them in a pile, product-side up.
- They should take it in turns to take a card from the pile.
- **The object of the game is to try to remember the name of the shop where you get that product.**
- If they remember correctly, they can keep the card.
- The player with most cards at the end is the winner.

GAME 2 Personalising
pairwork visualisation
- Ask the students to close their eyes and try to visualise the main street in their home town (or the town where they are studying). Can they remember all the shops?
- They should then open their eyes and tell their partner.

GAME 3 Communicating
small group information gap game
The shopping centre
- Put students in groups of 3-4.
- Give each group a set of maps. (For groups of three use maps 1-3.)
- Ask them to take one map each, and not to show it to anyone else.
- **The object of the game is to find the shops where you can buy the products on the shopping lists and mark them in on the map.**

- To do this, they will have to ask the other members of the group, 'Where's the ...?' and mark the shop in on their maps.

15 Shopping lists

Topic area
common household products

Vocabulary focus
chemist's: *aspirin, deodorant, cotton wool, film, perfume, plasters, shampoo, shaving foam, soap, suncream, tissues, toothpaste*

supermarket/minimarket/general store: *batteries, floor cleaners, light bulbs, plastic bags, polish, shoe polish, toilet rolls, washing powder, washing-up liquid*

stationer's: *envelopes, pen, sellotape, wrapping paper, writing paper*

newsagent's: *magazine, newspaper*

post office: *stamps*

Structures
be, have got, get, need, some/any

Materials and preparation

GAME 1 Copy the product cards. Don't forget to copy the names of the products on the back. You will need one set per pair of students.

GAME 2 None (though one set of product cards per pair of students might help them remember the products).

GAME 3 Copy and cut up one set of product cards and one set of task cards for each group of 3-4.

NOTE: If you don't feel your students need to learn all the words, simply select the cards you feel most appropriate for their level/culture. To reduce the vocabulary load for Game 3, either reduce the number of task cards, or tell the students to find fewer items (three, say, instead of six or seven for each task).

How to use the games

GAME 1 Memorising
pairwork sorting game

- Divide the students into pairs.
- Give each pair a set of product cards.
- Ask them to spread the cards out word-side up.
- Write up the names of five shops on the board: CHEMIST   NEWSAGENT   STATIONER   POST OFFICE   SUPERMARKET   (MINIMARKET/GENERAL STORE)
- **The object of the game is to sort the product cards into groups according to which shop sells them.**
- Students should work together to sort the cards into five piles – one for each shop.
- They can check if they are right by looking at the pictures on the back.

- When the cards are all picture-side up, they can see if they can remember all the words.

GAME 2 Personalising
pairwork guessing game

- Ask the students to think about their own houses: Have they run out of anything? What do they need to buy? Get them to write themselves a list.
- When they have finished, put them in pairs. They should tell each other which shop(s) they need to go to and their partner should try to guess the list.

GAME 3 Communicating
small group guessing game

Preparations

- Put the students in small groups of 3-4.
- Give them each a task card.
- Ask them to write themselves a shopping list for all the things they will need to complete the task. They can spread the pictures of products out on the table to remind themselves if they need to.
- When they have finished, they should read out their list to the group (without mentioning the task).
- **The object of the game is to guess what each task was.**

16 Containers

Topic area
containers for food and household products

Vocabulary focus
bag, bar, bottle, box, carton, jar, packet, pot, sachet, tin, tub, tube

Extra vocabulary
beer, chocolate, chocolates, cigarettes, crisps, glue, honey, ice cream, jam, margarine, matches, milk, mustard, orange juice, peas, potatoes, sauce, shampoo, soap, soup, tea, toothpaste, vinegar, yoghurt; out of stock, sold out

Structures
be, be like, have got; because clauses

Materials and preparation

GAME 1 Copy the product cards and the container cards. You will need one set of product cards and one set of container cards per pair of students.

GAME 2 No materials.

GAME 3 Mentally divide your class in half. Copy and cut up one set of container cards for each student in that group. Write a list of products and containers on the board for the others.

NOTE: If you don't feel your students need to learn all the words, simply select the cards you feel most appropriate for their level/culture, but make sure for every container card you select, there is at least one appropriate product card (e.g. if you choose to teach *bottle*, then you must also teach *beer* and/or *vinegar*; if you discard *tub*, then you must also discard *margarine* and *ice cream*).

How to use the games

GAME 1 Memorising
pairwork matching game

- Divide the students into pairs.
- Give each pair a set of product cards and a set of container cards.
- They should place the product cards face down in a pile in the middle, and shuffle and deal out the container cards. They can pick these up and look at them.
- The first player turns up a product card. The first player to match the product with a suitable container from his hand, shouting the name of container and product, can discard the pair of cards.
- **The object of the game is to match products with containers. (In some cases there is more than one possibility.)**
- The player to get rid of his cards first is the winner.

GAME 2 Personalising
pairwork discussion

- Write up this sentence:
  Life is like a ... .
- Complete it yourself in any way you like, e.g. 'Life is like a pot of honey', 'Life is like a sachet of sauce' and tell the students why (e.g. 'Because it tastes sweet' or 'Because there's never enough of it').
- Then get them to complete the sentence for themselves.
- Put them in pairs or small groups to share their sentences and reasons.
- Ask the whole class to volunteer examples.

GAME 3 Communicating
whole class collecting game

Out of stock

- Write up on the board a list of containers down one side and a list of items down the other.
- Divide the class in half.
- Give the students in one half a complete set of container cards each. Ask them to decide on a product for each container and to write it in on the container.
- Ask the students in the other half to write themselves a shopping list of six items chosen from the two lists on the board.
- Ask the first group of students to remain seated. They are the shops.
- Ask the second group to stand up. They are the shoppers.
- The shoppers should go round the shops asking for the items on their list. If they find a shop that stocks it, the shopkeeper should give them the card.
- Explain to them that some items they want might not be in stock or might be sold out.
- **The object of the game is to obtain as many items as possible.**
- The first person to get all the items is the winner.

17 Seasons, months, days of the week

Topic area
seasons, months, days

Vocabulary focus
names of the seasons, months and days of the week

Extra vocabulary
best, birthday, day, least, month, season; numbers (other items may be requested by students in Game 2)

Structures
be, be born, can, like; present simple, time prepositions (*in, on*), *because* clauses

Materials and preparation

GAME 1 Copy and cut up one set of season cards, month cards and day cards for each pair of students. Remember to copy the numbers on the back.

GAME 2 None.

GAME 3 No materials, though it is a good idea to bring a diary or calendar with you, or ask the students to do so.

How to use the games

GAME 1 Memorising
pairwork sorting and arranging games

- Divide the students into pairs.
- Give each pair a set of season, month and day cards.
- They should shuffle these together and then spread them out, word-side up on the table.
- **The object of the game is to sort the cards into three groups: *seasons, months, days*.**
- Students should take it in turns to assign a card to its group.
- When they have finished, they should try to arrange each group in chronological order.
- They can check if they are right at the end by turning each card over to see the number on the back. (They can also check if they have a card in the wrong group – the numbers have different typefaces for the seasons, months and days.)
- When all the cards are number-side up, they can see if they can remember the names.

GAME 2   Personalising
whole class search game

- Put up the following sentence frames on the board
  I like ... best because ... .
  I like ... least because ... .
- Ask students to complete the two sentences three times, once for each season, month and day.
- When they have done this, ask them to stand up and move around the class, trying to find someone who shares their opinions. (They don't have to find someone who shares all their preferences, just one person for each sentence!)

GAME 3   Communicating   **Long game**
whole class arranging game

Timelines

- Ask everyone in the class to stand up.

  The game is played in three parts, practising 1) seasons, 2) months, 3) dates.

  The parts are independent of each other – you don't have to do them all!

- **1. The object of the first part of the game is to find everyone who was born in the same season as they were and to stand together in a group.**
- To do this, they will have to move around the class asking 'What season were you born in?' or 'Were you born in spring/summer/autumn/winter?' and join up with everyone who shares the same season until the whole class is in four groups.
- When they have done this, go on to the second part of the game.
- **2. The object of the second part of the game is for them to form a long line, in order of birthdays.**
- To do this, they will have to move around the class asking 'When were you born?' or 'When is your birthday?' and arrange themselves in order of the months and days. Indicate where the head of the line should be.
- When they are in a line, check they are in the right order and go on to the third part of the game.
- **3. The object of the third part of the game is to group themselves according to what day their birthday falls on this year.**
- To do this, they will have to first work out what day their birthday will fall on this year, then move round the class asking 'What day is your birthday this year?' It is a good idea to have a calendar or diary available for consultation in this part of the game.

18 Weather

Topic area
weather

Vocabulary focus
bright, cloudy, cold, cool, dull, foggy, hot, icy, misty, rainy, showery, snowy, stormy, sunny, warm, windy

Extra vocabulary
none (though students may ask the names of the objects in Game 3: *suncream, sunglasses, umbrella, raincoat, foglamp, kite, oilskins, toboggan, skates, T-shirt, jumper, swimsuit, woolly hat*)

Structures
be, like + -ing, need, What ... like?

Materials and preparation

GAME 1   Copy and cut up one set of weather cards for each pair of students. (Don't forget to copy the words on the back.)

GAME 2   None.

GAME 3   Copy and cut up one set of weather cards (leave out *dull* and *cloudy*; you don't need to copy the words on the back) and one corresponding set of object cards for each student in the class.

NOTE: If you don't feel your students need to learn all the words, simply select the cards you feel most appropriate.

How to use the games

GAME 1   Memorising
pairwork matching game

- Divide the students into pairs.
- Give them the set of weather cards.
- They should spread these picture-side up on the table.
- **The object of the game is to remember the words on the back.**
- If a student remembers the word correctly, she can keep the card.
- The player with most cards at the end is the winner.
- Then they should spread the cards word-side up and try to group them into pairs: each card has a pair with almost the same meaning:
  rainy – showery, foggy – misty, windy – stormy, cloudy – dull, sunny – bright, cool – cold, hot – warm, snowy – icy

GAME 2   Personalising
pairwork guessing game

- Put up the following sentence frame:
  When it's ..., I like ... -ing.
- Ask the students to complete the sentence for the following types of weather: *rainy, foggy, windy, cloudy, sunny, cold, hot, snowy, stormy.*
- Then put them in pairs to guess each other's sentences.

GAME 3 Communicating
whole class matching game

Getting equipped

- Give each student in the class a weather card.
- Then give them each an object card. Make sure their object doesn't correspond to their weather card.
- **The object of the game is to find the right object for the weather.**
- To do this, they will have to get up and move around the class asking 'What's the weather like?' When they find someone with the weather card that corresponds to their object (e.g. *sunny – sunglasses*) they should give them the object (e.g. 'Then you'll need this!' 'Don't forget these!').
- When they have given away their original object and got the one they need, they should sit down.

19 Everyday actions

Topic area
daily actions

Vocabulary focus
brush, catch, come, cook, do the shopping, drink, drive, eat, fetch (from school), finish, get out of, get to, get up, go, have (breakfast/lunch/dinner/a shower), listen to, make, play, put on, read, ride, ring, shut, sleep, start, take (to school), talk, throw, turn off, wake up, wash, watch, write

Extra vocabulary
bathroom, bed, bike, breakfast, bus, car, coffee, dinner, door, downstairs, hair, kitchen, letters, lunch, radio, tea, teeth, time, TV, work (other food items can be added)

Structures
be, at ... o'clock; present simple

Materials and preparation

GAME 1 Copy and cut up two story cards and both sets of action cards per pair of students. (Don't forget to copy the words on the back.)

GAME 2 One set of action cards per pair of students.

GAME 3 Copy and cut up one set of action cards and one set of time cards per group of 3-4 students. (You don't need the words on the back.) There is a Rules sheet for this game at the back of the book. Make one copy per group.

NOTE: If you want to limit the vocabulary practised, just use one story and its set of action cards for Game 1. Use the same action cards for Games 2 and 3.

How to use the games

GAME 1 Memorising
pairwork arranging game

- Divide the students into pairs.
- Give each pair story card 1: Sanjay's day and its set of action cards (in muddled order).
- One student should take the story, the other should spread the cards out in front of her.
- The first student should read the story, while the second arranges the pictures in order to tell the story.
- **The object of the game is to get the pictures arranged in the same order as the story.**
- When they have finished, they can put the story away, and retell it from memory using the pictures. They can check as they go by turning the pictures over to see the words on the back.
- Then repeat the activity with story card 2: Lucy's day, with the second student telling the story this time.

GAME 2 Personalising
pairwork arranging activity

- Divide the students into pairs and give each pair a set of all the action cards.
- They should take it in turns to select and arrange cards to show a typical day, telling their partner about it as they do so.

GAME 3 Communicating
small group matching game

Make my day

- Divide the students into groups of 3-4.
- Give each group a set of all the action cards and a set of time cards.
- They should deal out the time cards and put the action cards in a pile face down in the middle of the table.
- One player should pick up an action card. If she can make a (plausible!) sentence about it using one of the time cards in her hand, e.g. 'I eat breakfast at 7 o'clock', she can discard the pair of cards (time and action). If she hasn't got an appropriate time card she must replace the action card at the bottom of the pile.
- Then it is the next player's turn.
- **The object of the game is to match up all the time cards in your hand with appropriate actions.**
- The player to get rid of all her cards first is the winner.

20 Work activities

Topic area
work actions

Vocabulary focus
build, catch, cook, cut, deliver (letters), design, do (experiments), draw, drive, fly (planes), grow, help, make (things), paint, pull out (teeth), put out (fires), repair (cars), sell, study, teach, type, write

Extra vocabulary

bus, cars, children, criminals, crops, fires, hair, houses, letters, machines, meals, newspaper reports, people, planes, plans, sick, teeth, things

Structures

be, would like, like + -ing; because clauses, present simple (especially third person and *Who* questions)

Materials and preparation

GAME 1   Copy and cut up one set of job pictures (from *Unit 3 Jobs*) and one set of verb cards per pair of students. (Don't forget the words on the back of the job pictures.)

GAME 2   No materials.

GAME 3   Copy and cut up two sets of job pictures (from *Unit 3*) per group of 3-4 students. (You don't need the words on the back.) There is a Rules sheet for this game at the back of the book. Make one copy per group.

NOTE: If you don't feel your class need to learn all the words, simply select the cards you feel are most appropriate for their level/culture. Make sure that every verb card you select has a matching job picture in Game 1.

How to use the games

GAME 1   Memorising

pairwork mime and matching games

1
- Divide the students into pairs.
- Give each a pile of verb cards. Ask them to place them face down in a pile in the middle of the table.
- The first student turns up a card without showing it to her partner and mimes the action.
- **The object of this part of the game is to guess the action being mimed.**
- When her partner guesses correctly, it is his turn to take a card.

2
- Then give each pair a pile of job pictures.
- They should spread these out on the table and put the verb cards face down in a pile again.
- They should take it in turns to turn up a verb from the verb pile.
- **The object of this part of the game is to match job and verb.**
- The first person to do this correctly, making a sentence (e.g. 'A pilot flies planes'), can keep the pair of cards. (Remind them about the 's' in the third person singular!)
- At the end, the person with the most cards is the winner.

GAME 2   Personalising

pairwork discussion

- Put up the following sentence frames on the board:
  I'd like to be a ... because I like ... .
  I wouldn't like to be a ... because I don't like ... .
- Ask students to complete the sentences for themselves. They can make as many sentences as they like. Set a time limit if you like.
- When the time is up, put them in pairs to share their opinions.

GAME 3   Communicating

small group quiz

Jobquiz

- Divide the students into groups of 3-4.
- Give each group two sets of job pictures from *Unit 3*.
- One student in each group is the Quizmaster. She takes one set of pictures and places them face down in front of her.
- The others should deal out the cards evenly amongst themselves. They can pick these up and look at them.
- The Quizmaster picks up the first card and asks a question, e.g. (picking up picture of a pilot) 'Who flies planes?'
- The player with the appropriate card answers and throws away the card.
- **The object of the game is to get rid of all the cards by answering questions correctly.**
- The player who gets rid of all his cards first is the winner.

21 Household tasks

Topic area
housework

Vocabulary focus
baking, cleaning, cooking, dusting, gardening, ironing, laying the table, making the beds, mending, polishing, shopping, sweeping, tidying up, vacuuming, washing, washing up

Structures
be, do (as in *do the shopping*), *like/hate/don't mind + -ing, I'll ...* (for offers)

Materials and preparation

GAME 1   Copy and cut up one set of word cards and one set of picture cards per pair of students.

GAME 2   None.

GAME 3   Copy and cut up one set of picture cards and one set of role cards per group of 3-4 students. There is a Rules sheet for this game at the back of the book. Copy one per group.

NOTE: If you don't feel your students need to learn all the words, simply select the cards you feel most appropriate for their level/culture. For Game 3, if there are items you don't want to practise, delete these from the role cards and make sure the corresponding item is not included in the pack of picture cards. (To be fair, you should delete the same number of items from each role card, otherwise some family members will end up doing more than their fair share of housework!)

How to use the games

GAME 1 Memorising
pairwork matching and miming games

1
- Divide the students into pairs and give each pair a set of word cards.
- Students should place these face down in a pile on the table.
- They should take it in turns to pick a card from the pile and mime the action to their partner.
- **The object of this part of the game is to guess the action being mimed.**
- If they guess correctly, they can keep the card.
- The winner is the player with most cards at the end.

NOTE: This can be done in two teams. Copy a pile of cards for each team. Members of the teams take it in turns to come and take a card and mime the action to their team. As soon as the team guesses, someone else can come and take a card.

2
- Now give each pair a set of picture cards.
- They should lay out the word cards and place the picture cards face down in a pile.
- **The object of this part of the game is to match words and pictures.**
- Players take it in turns to turn up a picture from the pile.
- The player who matches the picture with the right word first can keep the cards.
- The player with most cards at the end is the winner.

GAME 2 Personalising
group discussion

- Write up the following sentence frames on the board:
  I quite like ... -ing.
  I don't mind ... -ing.
  I hate ... -ing.
- Ask the students to complete the sentences according to which chores they like most, don't dislike or dislike most.
- Then put them in groups to share their opinions. Ask them which is the most popular and which the least popular chore in their group.
- Then get class totals by asking each group for its most and least popular activity.

GAME 3 Communicating
small group exchanging game

Division of labour

- Put the students in small groups of 3-4.
- Give each group a set of role cards and a set of picture cards.
- Each student should take a role card.
- Tell them that they all belong to the same family. The role card shows who they are. Their mother has decided the house is dirty. They are going to have to work together to spring-clean their house.
- They should deal out the cards equally. These are the chores Mum has given them to do.
- **The object of the game is for each student to end up doing chores he doesn't mind and to avoid those he doesn't like.**
- They will have to do this by asking others what chores they have, e.g. 'What have you got to do?' and then attempting to make bargains and swap their cards, e.g. 'You do the dusting, I'll do the washing up', 'You sweep the floors and I'll tidy up' etc.
- The game ends when they've all got the jobs they want. (If there are only three students in the group, however, there will be four jobs left that no one wants to do. The winner will be the player who has none, or fewest, of these.)

22 Hobbies

Topic area
names of hobbies and leisure activities

Vocabulary focus
camping, cards, chess, climbing, collecting stamps, computer games, cycling, dancing, fishing, gardening, gliding, knitting, music, painting, photography, pottery, reading, riding, sailing, sewing, walking, windsurfing, yoga

Extra vocabulary
free time, hobbies, present (students do not need to know the names of the pieces of equipment, though they might be interested to know some of them: *potter's wheel, brush and easel, cards, chess pieces, camera, spade, leotard, fishing rod, guitar and sheet of music, ballet shoes, book, plane, tent, saddle, bike, stamps, sewing machine, knitting needles, wool, walking boots, rope, ice axe, sails, surfboard, computer*)

Structures
be, have got, like + -ing, would like, want to, present simple (especially third person and *Who* questions)

Materials and preparation

GAME 1 Copy and cut up one set of hobby cards (words) and one set of equipment cards (pictures) per pair of students.

GAME 2 No materials.

GAME 3 Copy and cut up enough hobby cards for your students to have three each. Copy and cut up a matching equipment card for every hobby card.

NOTE: If you don't feel your students need to learn all the words, simply select the cards you feel most appropriate for their level/culture. For Game 3, you can limit vocabulary by giving students fewer hobby cards (one or two instead of three).

How to use the games

GAME 1 Memorising

pairwork matching games

- Divide the students into pairs.
- Give each pair a set of hobby cards and a set of equipment cards.
- They should spread the word cards (hobby cards) out on the table, face up, and place the pictures (equipment cards) face down in the middle.
- They should take it in turns to take a picture from the pile.
- **The object of the game is to match the equipment to the hobby.**
- The first player to find the right hobby card, saying the name of the hobby, may keep the pair of cards.
- At the end the player with most cards is the winner.

GAME 2 Personalising

small group discussion

- Put up the following sentence frames:
  I like ... .
  I don't like ... .
  I would like to try ... .
  I never want to try ... !
- Ask students to complete the four sentences.
- Then put students in small groups and ask them to guess each others' sentences.

GAME 3 Communicating

whole class exchanging and collecting game

Flea market

- Give each student in the class three hobby cards. Tell them these are their favourite hobbies.
- Then give each student three equipment cards. These should not match the hobby cards in their hand. Tell them this is some old equipment from a hobby they used to do.
- **The object of the game is for each student to find the appropriate pieces of equipment for his hobbies.**
- To do this, they should get up and move around the class, telling other people what their hobbies are, and asking about other people's hobbies, e.g. 'What are your hobbies?/What do you like doing in your free time?' 'I like ... / I'm interested in ...' .
- When they find someone who needs one of their pieces of equipment, they can give it to him, e.g. 'Oh really?/That's nice! I've got something here for you/Would you like this?/Would this be useful?' etc.
- When they have given away their useless equipment and got the equipment they need, they can sit down.

23 Sports

Topic area
names of sports

Vocabulary focus
athletics, badminton, boxing, cycling, football, handball, hockey, golf, gymnastics, judo, riding, rugby, running, sailing, skating, skiing, swimming, table tennis, tennis, volleyball

Extra vocabulary
playing, watching, interested (students do not need to know the names of the pieces of equipment, though they might be interested to know some of them: tennis racket, football, skis, ice skates, swimsuit, rugby ball, golf club, sails, hockey stick, hurdle, table tennis bat, badminton racket, saddle, boxing gloves, running shoes, bicycle, volleyball net, judo clothes, vaulting horse)

Structures
be, be good at, be interested in, can, like + -ing, would like ..., Let's ..., How about ...?

Materials and preparation

GAME 1 Copy and cut up one set of action cards and one set of equipment cards per pair or small group of students. Don't forget to copy the words on the back.

GAME 2 One set of action cards per pair.

GAME 3 Copy and cut up one set of action cards and one set of equipment cards for each group of three to four students. (You don't need the words on the back.) There is a Rules sheet for this game at the back of the book. Make one copy per group.

NOTE: If you don't feel your students need to learn all the words, simply select the cards you feel most appropriate for their level/culture.

How to use the games

GAME 1 Memorising

pairwork matching games

- Divide the students into pairs.
- Give each pair one set of equipment cards and one set of action cards.
- They should place the equipment cards face down in a pile and spread the action cards face up on the table.
- They should take it in turns to turn up a card from the equipment pile.
- **The object of the game is to match the equipment and the action.**
- The first person to find the matching action card, shouting the name of the sport (e.g. 'Tennis!'), can keep the pair of cards.
- At the end the player with most cards is the winner.

GAME 2   Personalising
small group discussion

- Put the following headings on the board:
  I LIKE   I LIKE WATCHING   I'M NOT INTERESTED IN
- Ask the students to put the sports in these three columns, according to personal preferences. (They can remind themselves of the sports by spreading the action cards out on the table.)
- When they have finished, put them in groups of 3-4 and ask them to see how many entries they have in common for each column.

GAME 3   Communicating
small group exchanging and collecting game

Anyone for tennis?

- Divide the students into groups of 3-4.
- Give each group a set of action cards and a set of equipment cards.
- They should shuffle the piles together and deal out six cards per person. The rest should be placed face down in a pile.
- The players can look at their hands of cards.
- **The object of the game is to find suitable equipment for all the action cards in their hands.**
- If they have any matching equipment and action cards already in their hands, they can lay them down as a 'trick'.
- Player 1 begins by choosing one of the action cards (e.g. *rugby*) in his hand and asking any other player, e.g. 'Would you like to (play rugby)?/Let's (play rugby)./How about (a game of rugby)?'
- If the second player has a rugby ball in his hand, he must give it to Player 1 and accept the offer, e.g. 'Great!/I'd love to.' If not, he must refuse, e.g. 'No, sorry, I can't play/I'm not very interested in rugby/I'm no good at rugby.'
- Player 1 may then lay down the two matching cards, or, if he did not get what he wanted, take another card from the pile in the middle.
- Then the turn passes to the next player.
- The winner is the player with most 'tricks' at the end.

24 Movements

Topic area
verbs of movement

Vocabulary focus
body: *bend, climb, crawl, fall, jump, kick, kneel, lie, run, sit, stand, swim, swing, turn, walk*

hand: *carry, catch, drop, give, hold, lift, pick up, pull, push, take, throw, touch, wave*

Extra vocabulary
baby, ball, beach, case, platform, rocks, shell, ticket, train, trolley

Structures
be, have got; simple present, present continuous

Materials and preparation

GAME 1   Copy and cut up one set of movement cards per pair of students. Don't forget the words on the back. You will need one small bag (paper or plastic) per group of 3-4 students in the second part of the game.

GAME 2   None.

GAME 3   Make one copy of each of the beach and station scenes.

NOTE: If you don't feel your students need to learn all the words, simply select the cards you feel most appropriate for their level/culture. To reduce the vocabulary load in Game 3, you will have to make a copy, tippex out the actions you don't want, then use this as your master.

How to use the games

GAME 1   Memorising
pairwork sorting and bingo games

1
- Divide the students into pairs and give each pair a set of movement cards.
- Ask them to lay out the cards word-side up.
- **The object of this part of the game is to sort them into two groups:** *hand movements* **and** *body movements*.
- They can check they are correct by turning the cards over to see the pictures.

2
- When they have finished, join the pairs into fours.
- They should leave one set of cards spread out on the table. Each player should select seven of these and lay them picture-side up in front of them.
- The other set of cards should be placed in a bag.
- Players take it in turns to put their hand in the bag and withdraw a card.
- Without showing it to the others, they should look at the picture and say the verb.
- If a player has the corresponding picture, she should ask for the card and place it on top of her own picture.
- **The object of this part of the game is to cover your cards first.**

GAME 2   Personalising
pairwork discussion

- Ask the students to spread the pictures out.
- Ask them to think back and write down the words (*stand, walk,* etc.) that they have done this week so far.
- Put them in pairs to compare lists.

25

GAME 3   Communicating

team guessing game

Where are we?

- Divide the class in two teams. (If you have more than, say, thirty students, it's probably best to do the activity in two groups of two teams.)
- Give one student in each team a picture (beach or station).
- That student should look at the picture and 'dictate' it to the others, i.e. describe the scene and the actions. ('A man is lying on the beach. A baby is crawling near him. A woman is running after the baby' etc.).
- As he describes, the others in the team should form a tableau according to his instructions. When the teams have finished they should each ask the other team 'Where are we?'
- **The object of the game is for each team to guess the other team's tableau.**
- When they have guessed correctly, give them a minute to study the other's tableau, then ask each team to reconstruct the others' tableau from memory.
- When they have reconstructed the tableau, they can look at the picture to see how accurately they have done it.

25 Shapes and patterns

Topic area

shapes and patterns

Vocabulary focus

shapes: *circle, diamond, oval, rectangle, semi-circle, square, triangle*

patterns: *checked, flowery, plain, spotted, starry, striped*

Extra vocabulary

(diamond)-shaped (household objects items may be requested by students in Game 2)

Structures

be, have got

Materials and preparation

GAME 1   Copy and cut up one set of object cards per pair of students.

GAME 2   None.

GAME 3   Copy and cut up two sets of flag cards per group of 3-4 students. There is a Rules sheet for this game at the back of the book. You will need one copy per group.

NOTE: If you don't feel your students need to learn all the words, simply select the cards you feel most appropriate for their level/culture.

How to use the games

GAME 1   Memorising

pairwork matching and collecting games

1

- Divide the students into pairs and give each pair a set of object cards.
- Get them to lay the cards out picture-side up.
- **The object of this part of the game is to collect matching pairs.**
- The players should take it in turns to pick up two cards from the table and say why they match.
- They can match two cards on any basis: shape or pattern, e.g. 'These are two triangles', 'These are both striped'.

2

- Now join the pairs into fours.
- Get them to put their two packs of cards together and shuffle them.
- The players deal out five cards each. The rest are placed face down in the middle.
- **The object of this part of the game is to collect sets of three cards.**
- The players look at their hands. If they have any three cards that form a set, they can lay these down as a 'trick'. Again, sets can be on a shape or pattern basis: three squares or three flowery objects for example.
- Player 1 begins by asking any other player for a card to complete a set, e.g. 'Have you got any triangles?' or 'Have you got anything spotted?'
- If the player has the card, she must give it to Player 1. If not, Player 1 takes a card from the pile.
- Then it is the next player's turn.
- The winner is the player with most 'tricks' at the end of the game.

GAME 2   Personalising

pairwork discussion

- Put up the following list on the board:

  Think of:

something triangular	something striped
something square	something spotted
something circular	something checked
something oval	something starry
something rectangular	something flowery
something diamond-shaped	something plain
something semi-circular	

  Ask the students to think of objects in their house at home.

- Circulate to deal with any vocabulary they need.
- Then put them in pairs to compare lists.

GAME 3 Communicating
small group matching game

The flag game

- Put the students in groups of 3-4 and give each group two sets of flag cards.
- Get them to shuffle the cards and deal out six cards to each player. They should place the rest in a pile face down.
- **The object of the game is to collect matching flags.**
- The players should look at their hands and lay down any matching pairs they have already as 'tricks'.
- Player 1 begins by asking any other player, 'Have you got a ...?' (e.g. a flag with a diamond inside a circle).
- If that player has that card, she must give it to Player 1 who can lay down the two matching cards together as a trick. If not, Player 1 must take another card from the pile.
- Then it is the next player's turn.
- The player who gets rid of her cards first is the winner.

26 Materials

Topic area
materials and substances

Vocabulary focus
bricks, cardboard, china, cotton, glass, gold, leather, metal, nylon, paper, plastic, rubber, silk, silver, stone, straw, wax, wood, wool

Extra vocabulary
belt, book, box, bracelet, candle, chair, comb, handkerchief, house, jumper, mat, mirror, path, plate, ring, scarf, spoon, tyre, umbrella, rooms of a house; *eat, wear, write* (students do not need to know, but may ask for, the objects in Game 1: *birthday card, boots, chain, cup, elastic band, earrings, knife, nightdress, plastic bag, sculpture, seal on a document, stamp, straw umbrella, table, tights, T-shirt, wall, wine glass, woolly hat*; vocabulary for household objects may also be requested by students in Game 2)

Structures
be, be made of; present simple

Materials and preparation

GAME 1 Copy and cut up one set of object (1) cards per pair of students. Don't forget the words on the back.

GAME 2 One set of object (1) cards per pair of students.

GAME 3 Copy and cut up one set of object (2) cards per group of 3-4 students.

NOTE: If you don't feel your students need to learn all the words, simply select the cards you feel most appropriate for their level/culture.

How to use the games
GAME 1 Memorising
pairwork matching game

- Divide the students into pairs.
- Give each pair a set of object (1) cards.
- Get them to spread these out on the table picture-side up.
- **The object of the game is to remember what each item is made of.**
- They should take it in turns to choose a card and say what the object is made of.
- They can check by turning the card over. If they are right, they can keep the card, if not, they must put it back.
- The player with most cards at the end is the winner.

GAME 2 Personalising
pairwork discussion

- Ask the students to spread out the object cards word-side up.
- Ask them to think of their own houses and to write down one thing in their house for each material. Circulate to supply any vocabulary they don't know.
- Then put them in pairs to compare lists.

GAME 3 Communicating
small group guessing game

Can you eat with it?

- Put the students into groups of 3-4.
- Give each a set of object (2) cards.
- Get them to put these in a pile face down.
- The first student takes a card from the pile but does not show it to the others.
- **The object of the game is for the others to guess the object.**
- They can do this by asking, 'Is it made of ...?', 'Can you eat with it/write with it/wear it?', 'Do you use it in the kitchen/living room/bathroom/bedroom/street?' etc.
- The player who guesses first can keep the card and take the next card.
- The player with most cards at the end is the winner.

NOTE: You can make the game easier if you think your students won't know the names of all the objects, by getting them to spread the cards out picture-side up, instead of keeping them in a pile. Check they know the names of all the objects. Then either play the game as above, or keep the pictures spread out and get the players to choose a card mentally without saying which one it is, instead of picking from the pile.

27 Town features

Topic area
town buildings

Vocabulary focus
bank, bus station, café, car park, church/mosque/temple, cinema, concert hall, football ground, hospital, hotel, library, market, office block, park, police station, post office, prison, pub, railway station, restaurant, school, shopping centre, skating rink, sports stadium, swimming pool, theatre, town hall

Extra vocabulary
beer, books, borrow, bus, buy, car, catch, coffee, criminals, eat, films, football, French, get married, go, learn, leave, listen, music, play, plays, post letters, pray, running, see, sick, skating, sleep, swimming, trains, trouble, walk, fruit and vegetables

Structures
can, there is/are; place prepositions (*at the end of, behind, in front of, next to, on the right/left, opposite*), imperatives (directions), present simple/infinitive of common verbs

Materials and preparation

GAME 1 Copy and cut up one set of building cards and one set of activity cards for each pair in your class. Don't forget the words on the back of the building cards.

GAME 2 No materials.

GAME 3 Copy and cut up one set of building cards and one set of direction cards. This will be enough for up to twenty-five students. If you have more, copy another set and play the game in two groups. If you have fewer, use the direction cards in the order in which they are printed, and choose picture cards to match.

NOTE: If you don't feel your students need to learn all the words, simply select the cards you feel most appropriate for their level/culture in Game 1 (making sure every building card you choose has a matching activity card). If you want to play Game 3 with a reduced vocabulary load, either use only half the street, starting from the station end, or make your own version. (Draw yourself a plan first, then write the cards.)

How to use the games

GAME 1   Memorising
pairwork matching game

- Divide the students into pairs.
- Give each pair a set each of building cards and activity cards.
- They should place the building cards picture-side up all over the desk, and place the activity cards in a pile face down.
- They should take it in turns to draw an activity card and to match it with the appropriate building card, trying to remember the name of the place.
- If they remember the name correctly, they may keep the building and the activity card. If not, their partner is allowed to have a guess.

- **The object of the game is to match all building and activity cards correctly.**
- The player with the most at the end is the winner.

GAME 2   Personalising
pairwork visualisation

- Ask the students to close their eyes and to imagine a walk in their home town.
- They should imagine a route that will take them past some of the places they have learnt and try to remember the name in English.
- When they have finished, ask them to draw a rough sketch of their walk and then either to write about it or describe the walk to their partner.

GAME 3   Communicating   `Long game`
whole class arranging game

We are a map

1
- One set of building cards and one set of direction cards is enough for twenty-seven students. If you have more than twenty-seven, use two sets and play the game in two groups. If you have fewer than twenty-seven students, use the direction and building cards in the following order: *railway station, bank, library, cinema, post office, school, concert hall, theatre, hotel, town hall, shopping centre, restaurant, pub, church/mosque/temple, hospital, café, police station, swimming pool, skating rink, bus station, park, prison, sports stadium, car park, football ground, office block, market.*
- Choose whether you are going to have a church/mosque/temple (according to your students' culture) in your street. Choose the appropriate picture and delete the two you haven't chosen from the building cards.
- Ask the students to come up to the front and stand with their backs to you. Pin one picture on each student's back (or use Blu-Tack).
- **The object of this part of the game is for each student to find out where they are by asking questions, e.g. 'Can I borrow books there?', 'Can I eat there?' etc.**
- They should move around asking and answering questions until they have found out where they are.
- When they have found out where they are, they should come and tell you.
- Check they are right by looking at their picture, and give them the appropriate direction card for their place.
- Ask them to sit down and wait for the second half of the game.

2
- When everyone is sitting down again, check that they all have a direction card, then start the second half of the game.
- Make a 'street' in the class – a long area with enough room for two rows of eight students opposite each other

with four students behind each row, e.g. a central aisle between desks or a long space at the front of the room.
- Tell the students which is the 'far' end of the street and which is the left-hand and right-hand side.
- **The object of this part of the game is for the students to find out where they are in the street and to place themselves in the correct position.**
- To do this, they will have to move around the room asking other students for information about where places are, until they find who they are next to, behind, in front of or opposite.
- They should then go and stand in that position.
- When everyone is in position, check that they are in the right place against this plan.

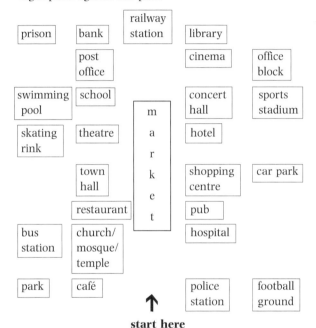

start here

NOTE: If you prefer to play the game in small groups, divide the students into groups of 3-4 and give each group a set of building cards and a set of direction cards. They should spread out the building cards and put the direction cards face down in a pile. They should turn up one card at a time and use the information to try to arrange the pictures into a 'street'.

28 Street features

Topic area
objects in the street

Vocabulary focus
bus shelter, bus stop, crossroads, drain, kerb, lamp-post, letterbox, litterbin, pavement, road, telephone box, traffic island, traffic lights, zebra crossing

Structures
Mind (the lamp-post!), there is/are; place prepositions

Materials and preparation

GAME 1
1 Copy the street feature labels and also the landscape feature labels from *Unit 30*. You will need one set of each per pair of students.

2 Copy the street feature labels and street picture 1. You will need one picture and one set of labels per pair.

GAME 2 No materials.

GAME 3 Copy street pictures 1 and 2. You will need a set of two pictures per pair of students.

NOTE: If you don't feel your students need to learn all the words, simply select the cards you feel most appropriate for their level/culture. In Game 3, the minimum necessary vocabulary is: *letterbox, zebra crossing, traffic lights, lamp-post, bus stop, telephone box* and *litterbin*, so if you intend to finish off with Game 3, your vocabulary selection in Game 1 should include these items.

How to use the games

GAME 1   Memorising
pairwork sorting and labelling games
- Divide the students into pairs.

1
- Give out the street features and landscape features labels.
- Ask the students to sort them into two groups: street and landscape.

2
- Give each pair a copy of street picture 1.
- Ask them to take it in turns to place a street label in the right place on the picture. They can check if they're right by turning the label over to see if the numbers correspond.
- **The object of the game is to label all the features correctly.**
- When they have finished and all the labels are number-side up, they can try to remember all the names of the features.

GAME 2   Personalising
pairwork visualisation
- Ask the students to close their eyes and imagine walking along a familiar route home (e.g. from the bus stop to their house).
- Then put them in pairs.
- Ask them to take it in turns to guide the other along the route. They should imagine the person is blind and does not know the way. They will need to help him by telling him where everything is, e.g. 'We're at the traffic lights now. We're going to cross the road. Here's the kerb.'
- If you have enough space, you can ask students to get up and walk around to enact the route, one leading and talking to the other (who keeps her eyes closed or is blindfolded!)

GAME 3 Communicating
pairwork information gap

Mind the lamp-post!

- Divide the students into pairs.
- Give one student in each pair street picture 1 and the other street picture 2.
- They should not look at each other's pictures.
- They should describe their pictures to each other.
- **The object of the game is to find seven differences between the two pictures.**

29 Places to live

Topic area
types of housing

Vocabulary focus
attic, basement, bungalow, caravan, castle, cave, cottage, detached house, farm, flat, hotel, houseboat, hut, igloo, lighthouse, palace, semi-detached house, space station, tent, terraced house, windmill

Extra vocabulary
big, cheerful, cold, comfortable, cosy, country, damp, dark, gloomy, light, small, spacious, town, warm, etc.

Structures
be, need, prefer, would like

Materials and preparation

GAME 1 Copy and cut up one set of house pictures for each group of 3-4 in your class.

GAME 2 No materials.

GAME 3 Copy and cut up one set of house pictures and one set of people cards for each group of 3-4 students.

NOTE: If you don't feel your students need to learn all the words, simply select the cards you feel most appropriate for their level/culture. In Game 3, make sure the people cards you select correspond with your selection of house pictures. And include one or two strange ones even if your students don't need them – it makes the game more fun!

How to use the games

GAME 1 Memorising
small group guessing game

- Divide the students into small groups of 3-4.
- Give each pair a set of house pictures.
- They should place these face down in a pile in the middle of the table.
- They should take it in turns to pick a card from the top. They should not show the card to anyone.
- The student with the card can give a clue by describing the house, e.g. 'It's small and cold. It's in the country.'
- The others can guess, e.g. 'Is it an igloo?' 'Is it a farm?'
- The student who guesses correctly can keep the card.
- Then it is the next player's turn.
- **The object of the game is to guess as many places as possible.**
- The student with the most cards at the end is the winner.

GAME 2 Personalising
pairwork discussion

- Put up the following headings on the board:
  COMFORTABLE   UNCOMFORTABLE   FUN
  TO LIVE IN   TO LIVE IN   TO LIVE IN
- Ask the students to complete the chart with names of places, according to their personal opinions.
- Then put them in pairs to share their views, e.g. 'I'd like to live in an igloo.' 'Oh no! It's too cold!'

GAME 3 Communicating
whole class or small group matching game

The igloo of my dreams

1
- If you are playing with the whole class, you will need five people cards and the corresponding five house cards per person. Get these ready, then shuffle the two piles together and deal out five cards to everyone in the class.
- **The object of this part of the game is for everyone to find suitable house cards for the people in their hand.**
- To do this, they will have to move around the class asking for the houses they need, e.g. 'I need a small detached igloo.' 'Have you got a nice cave?' until everyone has matched people and houses.

2
- If you want to play the game in small groups, divide the class into groups of 3–4 and give each group a set of house cards and a set of people cards.
- They should shuffle the two piles together and deal out eight to each player.
- **The object of this part of the game is for each player to find suitable houses for the people in his hand.**
- He can do this by asking other players, 'Have you got a ...?' If they have the card he needs, they must give it to him and he can discard the matching pair (house and person). If not, he takes a card from the pile and the turn passes to the next player.
- The winner is the player with most matching pairs at the end.

30 The countryside

Topic area
landscape features

Vocabulary focus
beach, cliff, fence, field, forest, gate, hedge, hill, lake, marsh, mountain, path, pond, river, road, stream, valley, village, wood

Structures
be, there is/are; place prepositions

Materials and preparation

GAME 1 Copy one countryside picture and one set of landscape labels per small group of three to four.

GAME 2 No materials.

GAME 3 Copy four countryside pictures and twelve sheep for each group of 3-4 students.

NOTE: If you don't feel your students need to learn all the words, simply select the cards you feel most appropriate for their level/culture. In Game 3, since the picture contains all the landscape features, you will have to tell the students to put their sheep only in a place they can name.

How to use the games

GAME 1 Memorising
small group labelling game

- Divide the students into groups of 3-4.
- Give each group a countryside picture and a set of landscape labels.
- They should put the picture where they can all see it and put the labels face down in a pile in the middle.
- They should take it in turns to pick up a card from the pile.
- The first person to say the number on the picture corresponding to the word on the card, can keep the card.
- **The object of the game is to match all the words with the numbers on the picture.**
- At the end the person with most cards is the winner.
- Check by putting up a key on the board at the end.

GAME 2 Personalising
pairwork visualisation

- Ask the students to close their eyes.
- Ask them to think of their favourite country view and to visualise it in their mind.
- Give them a little time to do this, then ask them to open their eyes and describe the view to a partner.

GAME 3 Communicating
small group guessing game

Lost sheep

- Divide the students into groups of 3-4.
- Give each student a countryside picture and three or four sheep.
- They can put their sheep anywhere they like on their picture, but must not show the others. Suggest they use a book as a barrier to prevent the others seeing.
- **The object of the game is to find out where the other people's sheep are.**
- They can do this as a guessing game, taking it in turns to ask each other about their sheep, e.g. 'Is there a sheep on the hill? Is it in the hedge? In the lake? By the fence?' etc.
- The student who guesses correctly can keep the sheep he 'found'.
- The winner is the one with most sheep at the end.

The photocopiable games material follows on pages 32 to 119

1 Family members

PICTURES

1 Family members

RELATIONSHIPS (1) (sentences)

Barbara is Susan's mother.	Tom is Susan's husband.	Charlie is Susan's brother.	Jill is Charlie's wife.
Michael is Laura's cousin.	Patrick is Tom's son.	Barbara is Laura's grandmother.	George is Patrick's grandfather.
Susan is Laura's aunt.	Charlie is Michael's uncle.	George is Charlie's father.	Laura is Patrick and Michael's cousin.
Susan is Charlie's sister.	Laura is Susan's niece.	Patrick and Michael are Charlie's nephews.	George and Barbara have two grandsons and a granddaughter.

1 Family members

RELATIONSHIPS (2) (names)

Jill – Charlie	Charlie – Susan	Tom – Susan	Barbara – Susan
George – Patrick	Barbara – Laura	Patrick – Tom	Michael – Laura
Laura – Patrick and Michael	George – Charlie	Charlie – Michael	Susan – Laura
George and Barbara – Patrick, Michael and Laura	Patrick and Michael – Charlie	Laura – Susan	Susan – Charlie

1 Family members

1 Family members

FAMILY TREE 1

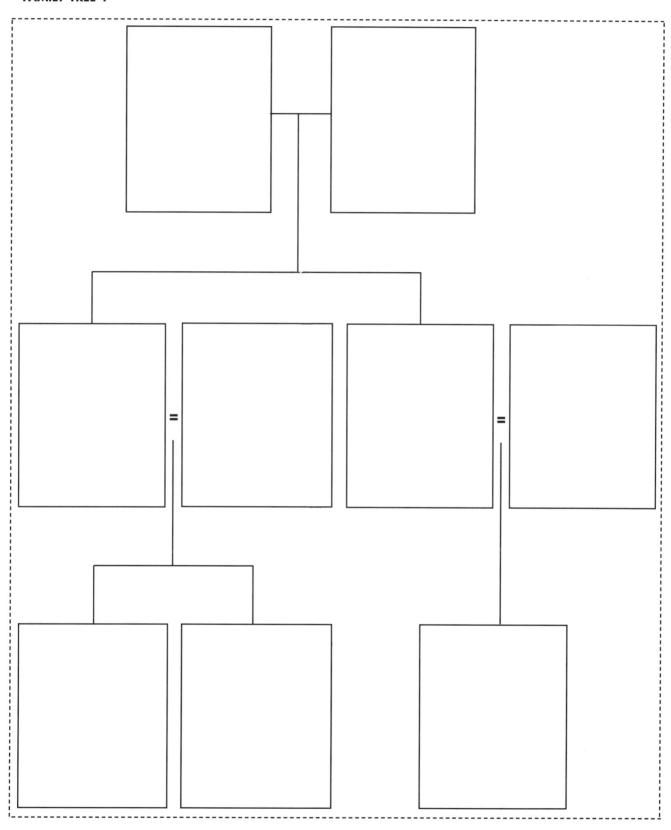

1 Family members

FAMILY TREE 2

2 Countries and nationalities

COUNTRIES (1)

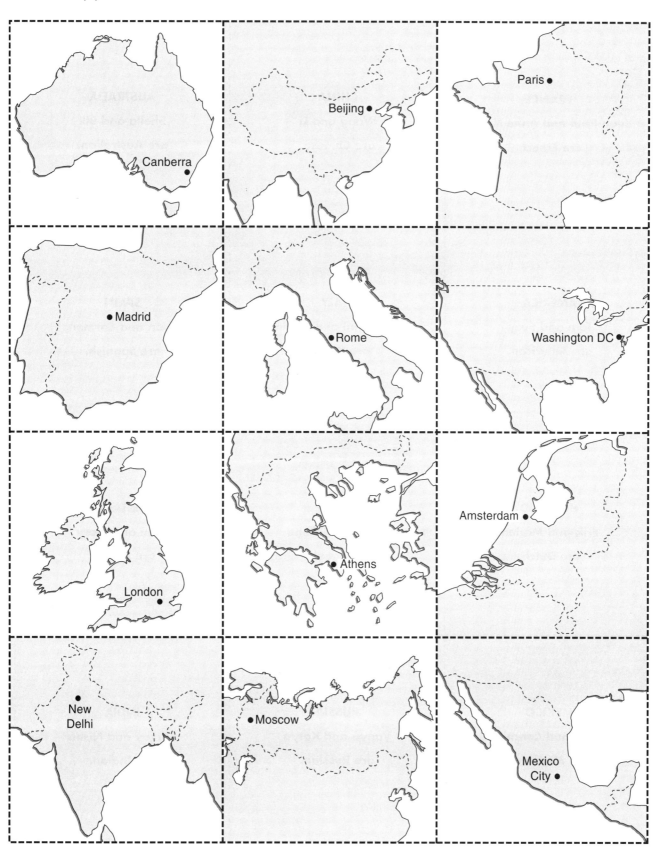

2 Countries and nationalities

COUNTRIES (2)

FRANCE Jean-Paul and Anne-Marie are French.	**CHINA** Wang and Li are Chinese.	**AUSTRALIA** Sheila and Bill are Australian.
AMERICA Tom and Suzy are American.	**ITALY** Giovanni and Maria are Italian.	**SPAIN** Juan and Carmen are Spanish.
HOLLAND Erik and Marion are Dutch.	**GREECE** Panos and Elena are Greek.	**BRITAIN** John and Mary are British.
MEXICO Pablo and Conchita are Mexican.	**RUSSIA** Vanya and Katya are Russian.	**INDIA** Sanjay and Nisha are Indian.

Elementary Vocabulary Games
Addison Wesley Longman   © J Hadfield 1998

2 Countries and nationalities

PEOPLE (1)

2 Countries and nationalities

PEOPLE (2)

Elementary Vocabulary Games
Addison Wesley Longman © J Hadfield 1998

3 Jobs

PICTURES (1)

3 Jobs

NAMES (1)

builder	artist	architect
car mechanic	businessman	bus driver
doctor	dentist	chef
farmer	factory worker	engineer

3 Jobs

PICTURES (2)

3 Jobs

NAMES (2)

journalist	hairdresser	firefighter
police officer	pilot	nurse
secretary	scientist	postman
teacher	student	shop assistant

5 Parts of the body

BODY PICTURES

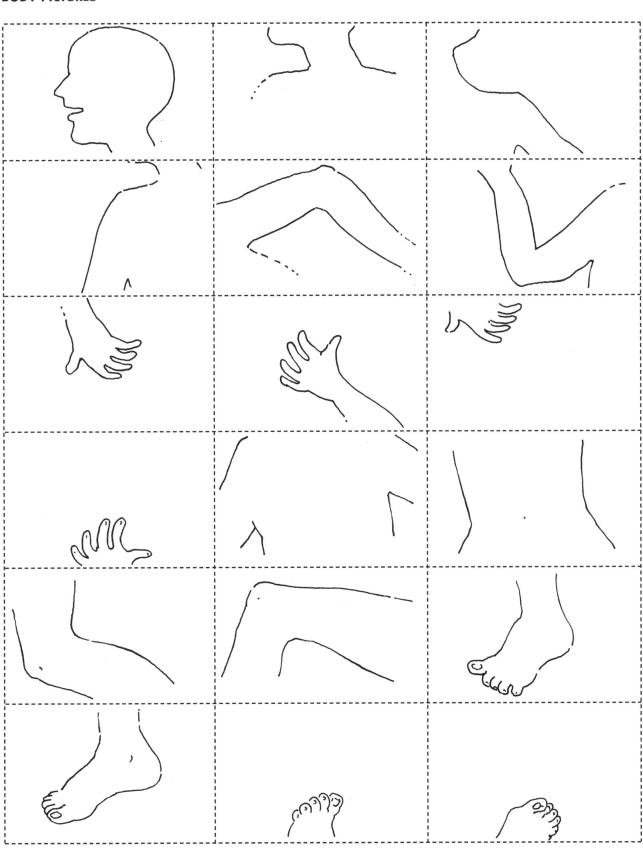

47

5 Parts of the body

BODY PICTURES (words)

shoulder	neck	head
arm	arm	shoulder
fingers	hand	hand
stomach	chest	fingers
foot	leg	leg
toes	toes	foot

5 Parts of the body

5 Parts of the body

ROBOT GAME

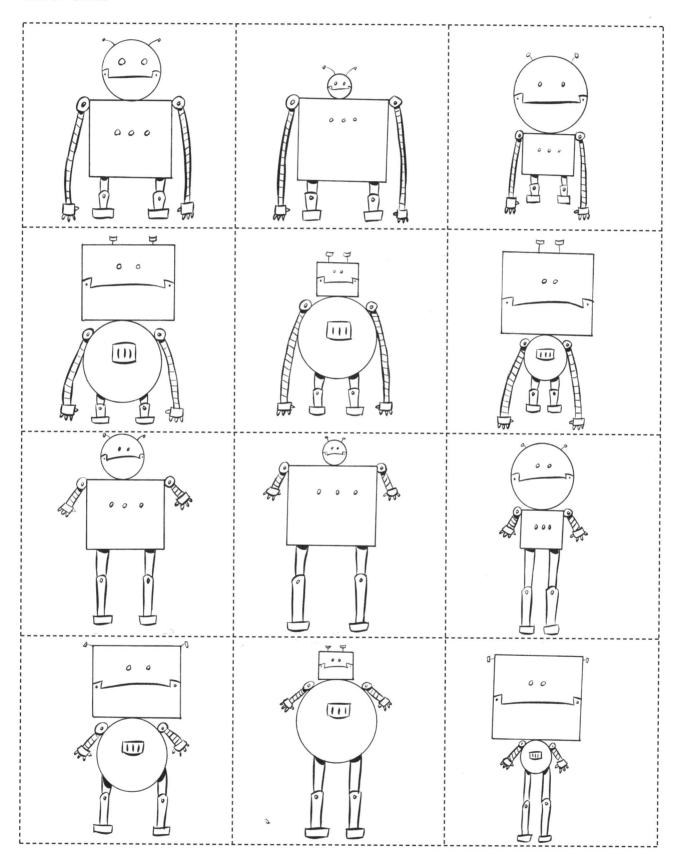

6 Faces

WORD COLLOCATIONS

long	long	long	short	hair	hair	hair	hair
short	curly	straight	straight	hair	hair	hair	hair
big	big	big	big	eyes	eyes	eyes	eyes
big	small	small	small	eyes	eyes	eyes	eyes
small	small	round	round	nose	nose	nose	nose
round	round	pointed	pointed	nose	nose	mouth	mouth
pointed	square	square	brown	chin	chin	chin	ears
brown	black	black	blue	ears	ears	face	face
green	blonde	red	thin	face	face	face	face

6 Faces

FACIAL FEATURES (pictures)

6 Faces

FACIAL FEATURES (words)

mouth	hair
eyelashes	nose
lips	teeth
moustache	beard
chin	eyebrows
forehead	cheeks
ears	eyes

6 Faces

FUNNY FACES

Elementary Vocabulary Games
Addison Wesley Longman   © J Hadfield 1998

7 Clothes

WASHING LINE GAME

7 Clothes

PICTURES

7 Clothes

WORDS

shorts	socks	skirt	jumper	T-shirt
swimsuit	pants	trousers	shirt	pyjamas
anorak	dress	blouse	vest	scarf
tie	gloves	tights	woolly hat	jacket
tracksuit	bra	trainers	suit	shoes
dressing gown	coat	slippers	leggings	jeans

8   Rooms in a house

ROOMS

attic	bathroom	bedroom	dining room	garage	garden
hall	kitchen	landing	living room	stairs	study
toilet	basement	cellar	first floor	ground floor	second floor

8   Rooms in a house

HOUSE PLANS

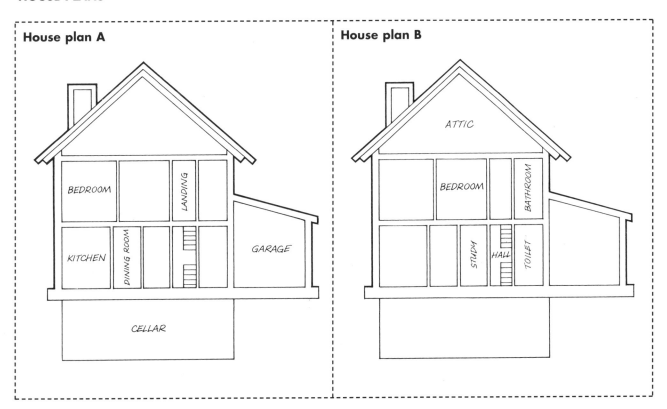

9 Furniture

FLAT PLAN

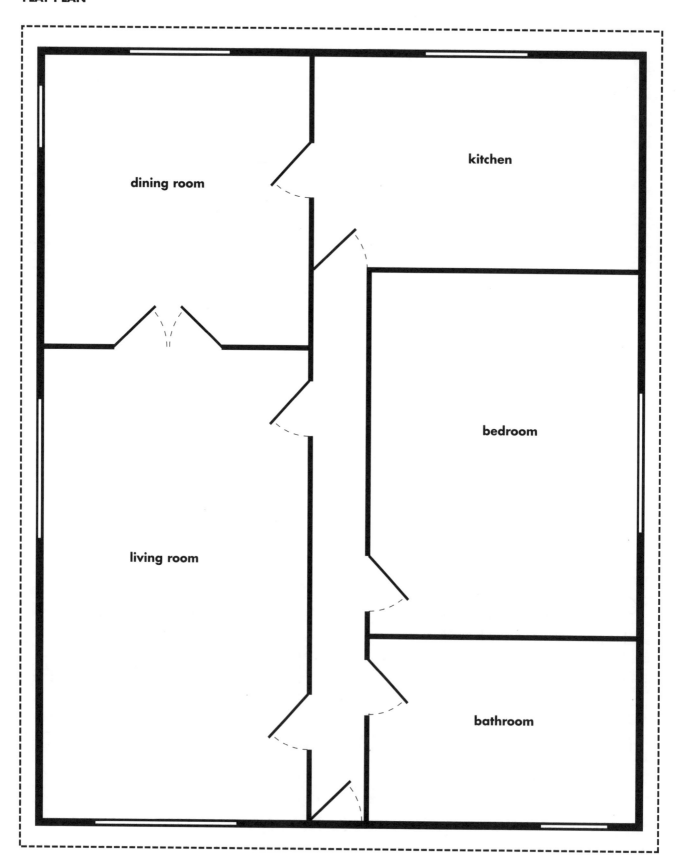

9 Furniture

FURNITURE CARDS (pictures)

9 Furniture

FURNITURE CARDS (words)

washing machine	sink	fridge	cupboard	cooker
sofa	desk	coffee table	bookcase	armchair
table	sideboard	rug	lamp	chairs
wardrobe	mirror	dressing table	chest of drawers	bed
washbasin	toilet	shower	bathroom cabinet	bath

9 Furniture

ROOM PLANS

10 Household objects

HOUSE PLAN

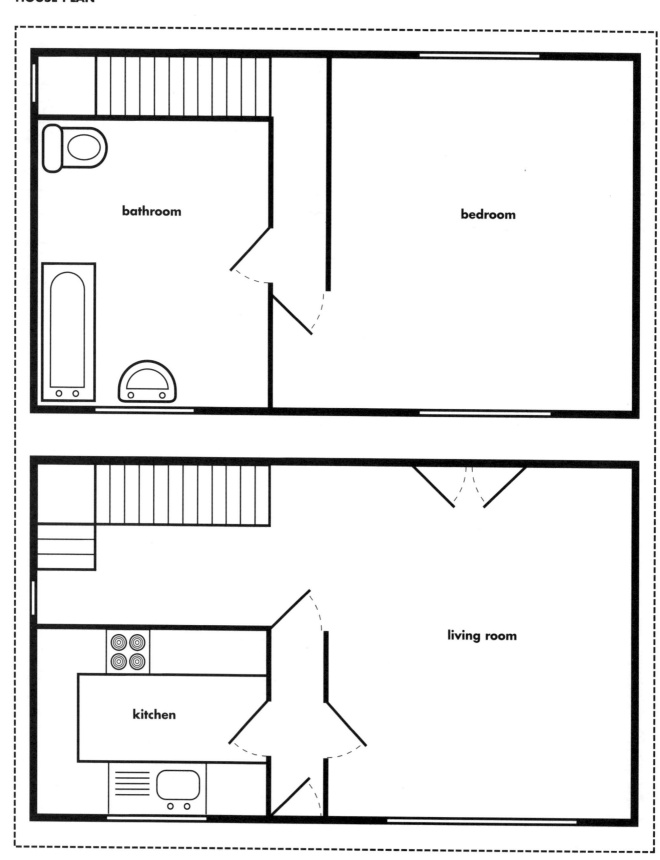

10 Household objects

PICTURES

63

10 Household objects

WORDS

alarm clock	hairdryer	duvet	blanket	sheet	pillow
towel	toothbrush	scales	razor	facecloth	bathmat
tray	tablecloth	radio	pedal bin	tablemats	clock
video	vase	TV	picture	hi-fi system	cushion

10 Household objects

ROOM PLANS

11 Kitchen objects

HOUSEWORK GAME

| 1 Lay the table. | 2 Make tea and coffee. | 3 Do the washing and ironing. | 4 Wash up the pans. | 5 Clean and hoover the floors. |

11 Kitchen objects

11 Kitchen objects

PICTURES

Elementary Vocabulary Games
Addison Wesley Longman © J Hadfield 1998

11 Kitchen objects

WORDS

spoon	plate	knife	glass	fork	bowl
teapot	saucer	kettle	jug	cup	coffeemaker
soap powder	laundry basket	ironing board	iron	clothes pegs	clothes horse
washing-up bowl	teatowel	saucepan	plate rack	frying pan	dishcloth
scrubbing brush	mop	hoover	dustpan and brush	bucket	broom

12 Food and drink

PICTURES

12 Food and drink

WORDS

beer	coffee	milk	orange juice	tea
wine	bacon	beef	biscuits	bread
butter	cake	cheese	chicken	cooking oil
eggs	fish	flour	ham	ice cream
jam	lamb	pork	rice	soup
spaghetti	sugar			

13 Fruit and vegetables

PICTURES

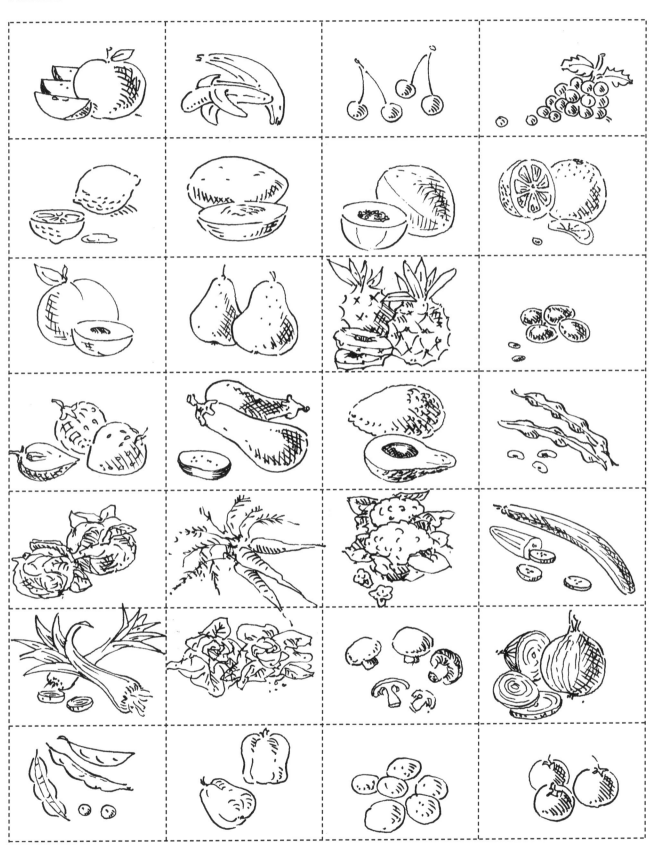

71

13 Fruit and vegetables

WORDS

grapes	cherries	bananas	apples
oranges	melons	mangoes	lemons
plums	pineapples	pears	peaches
beans	avocados	aubergines	strawberries
cucumbers	cauliflowers	carrots	cabbages
onions	mushrooms	lettuces	leeks
tomatoes	potatoes	peppers	peas

14 Shops

PICTURES

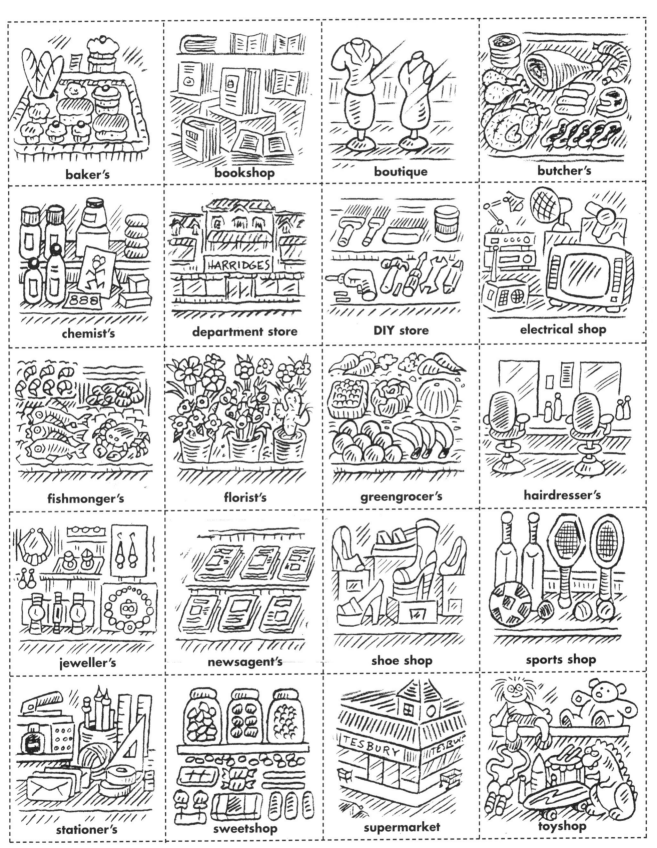

14 Shops

PRODUCTS

Elementary Vocabulary Games
Addison Wesley Longman © J Hadfield 1998

14 Shops

MAPS

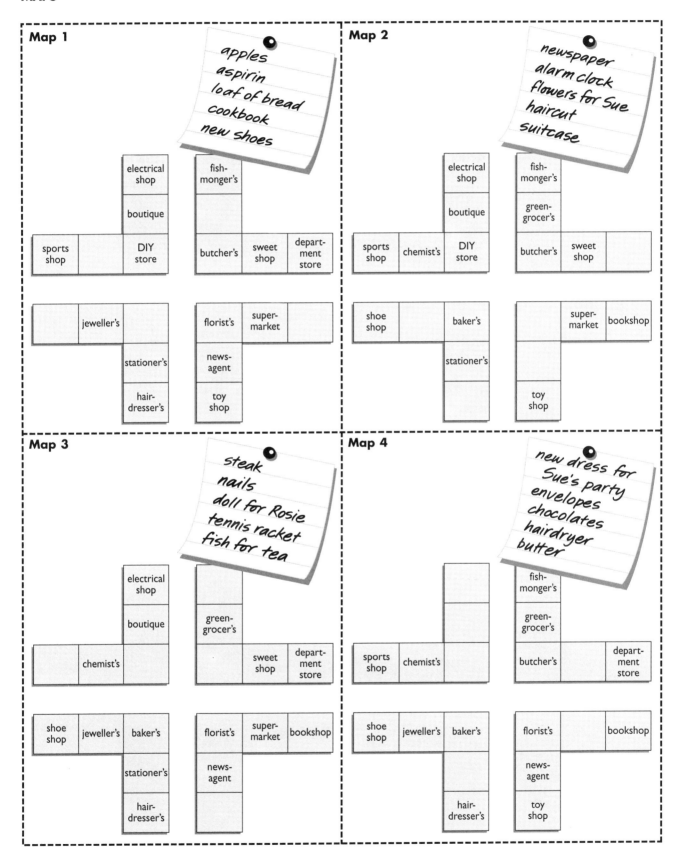

15 Shopping lists

TASKS

1	2	3	4
You are going to spring-clean the house.	You are going away on holiday.	You are going to a wedding.	You are going on a train journey. You want to read and get some letters done.

Elementary Vocabulary Games
Addison Wesley Longman © J Hadfield 1998

15 Shopping lists

PRODUCTS (pictures)

15 Shopping lists

PRODUCTS (words)

perfume	film	cotton wool	deodorant	aspirin
suncream	soap	shaving foam	shampoo	plasters
light bulbs	floor cleaner	batteries	toothpaste	tissues
washing powder	toilet rolls	shoe polish	polish	plastic bags
string	sellotape	pen	envelopes	washing-up liquid
stamps	newspaper	magazine	writing paper	wrapping paper

16 Containers

PICTURES

16 Containers

PRODUCTS

beer	chocolate	chocolates	cigarettes
crisps	glue	honey	ice cream
jam	margarine	matches	milk
mustard	orange juice	peas	potatoes
sauce	shampoo	soap	soup
tea	toothpaste	vinegar	yoghurt

16 Containers

Elementary Vocabulary Games
Addison Wesley Longman   © J Hadfield 1998

17 Seasons, months, days of the week

NAMES (1)

spring	summer	autumn	winter
January	February	March	April
May	June	July	August
September	October	November	December
Monday	Tuesday	Wednesday	Thursday
Friday	Saturday	Sunday	

17 Seasons, months, days of the week

NAMES (2)

4	3	2	1
4	3	2	1
8	7	6	5
12	11	10	9
4	3	2	1
	7	6	5

18 Weather

PICTURES

18 WEATHER

WORDS

cool	cold	cloudy	bright
icy	hot	foggy	dull
snowy	showery	rainy	misty
windy	warm	sunny	stormy

18 Weather

OBJECTS

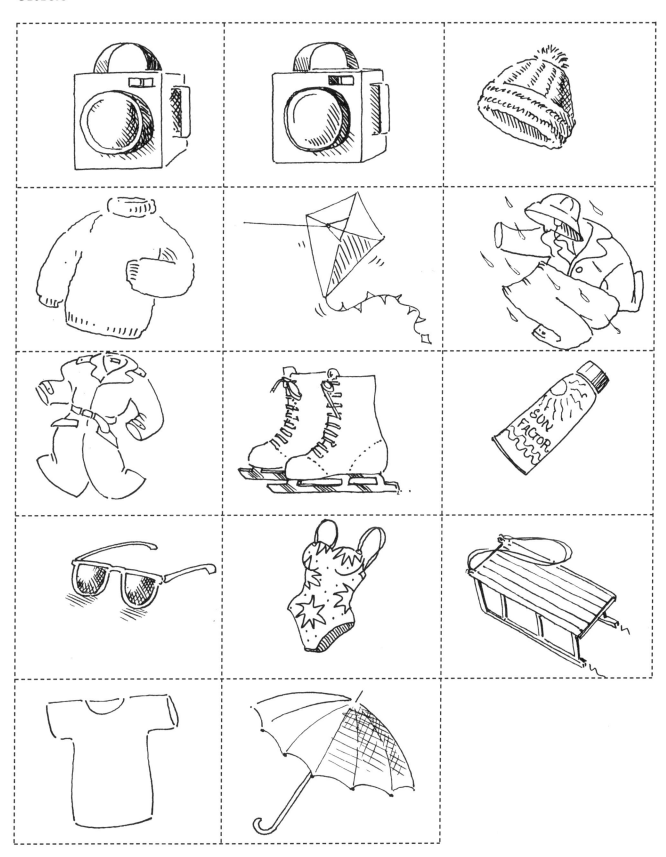

Elementary Vocabulary Games
Addison Wesley Longman © J Hadfield 1998

19 Everyday actions

STORIES

Story 1 Sanjay's Day
Sanjay's alarm clock rings at 7.00, but he usually turns over and goes back to sleep because he's tired. Sometimes, he throws the alarm clock across the room. So he wakes up late and runs into the bathroom to wash and brush his teeth. He doesn't have time to have a shower. He goes downstairs and turns the radio on to listen to music while he has breakfast. He doesn't have time to eat and he has to drink his tea in a hurry, because he's always so late. He leaves the house and runs to the bus stop to catch his bus. He gets to college at 9.00 (well, usually at 9.20!) and finishes at 4.00.

He comes home at about 4.30 and has dinner. After dinner, he sometimes watches TV, but he usually goes out with friends. He comes home late – 2 or 3 o'clock sometimes – and goes to bed and sleeps at once.

Story 2 Lucy's Day
Lucy gets up at 2 o'clock in the afternoon. She has a shower and has a late lunch. Then she does the shopping and fetches the kids from school. She plays with the children and then cooks dinner for everyone. When the children are in bed, she watches TV or writes letters or reads a book. Then it's time to go to work. She puts on her uniform and drives to work. She starts work at 10.00 at night and works until 6.00 in the morning. She comes home at about 6.30 and makes breakfast for everyone. Her husband takes the children to school and Lucy goes to bed – at 8 o'clock in the morning.

19 Everyday actions

TIME CARDS

6.00	6.30	7.00	7.30	8.00	8.30
9.00	9.30	10.00	10.30	11.00	11.30
12.00	12.30	1.00	1.30	2.00	2.30
3.00	3.30	4.00	4.30	5.00	5.30

19 Everyday actions

ACTIONS (1)

Elementary Vocabulary Games
Addison Wesley Longman   © J Hadfield 1998

19 Everyday actions

SENTENCES (1)

He runs into the bathroom to wash.	So he wakes up late.	Sometimes he throws the alarm clock across the room.	Sanjay's alarm clock rings at 7.00. But he usually turns over and goes back to sleep because he's tired.
He doesn't have time to eat and has to drink his tea in a hurry, because he's always so late.	He turns the radio on to listen to music.	He doesn't have time to have a shower. He goes downstairs.	He brushes his teeth.
He gets to college at 9.00 (well, usually at 9.20!).	He catches the bus.	He runs to the bus stop.	He leaves the house.
After dinner he sometimes watches TV.	He has his dinner.	He comes home at about 4.30.	He finishes college at 4.00.
He goes to sleep at once.	He goes to bed.	He comes home late – 2 or 3 o'clock sometimes.	Usually he goes out with friends.

19 Everyday actions

ACTIONS (2)

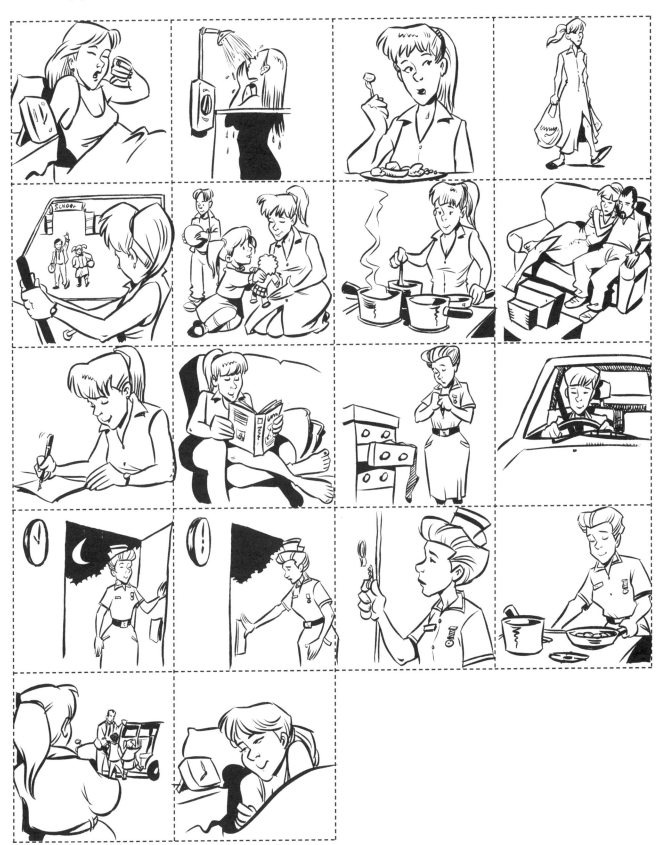

19 Everyday actions

SENTENCES (2)

Then she does the shopping.	She has a late lunch.	She has a shower.	Lucy gets up at 2 o'clock in the afternoon.
When the children are in bed she watches TV.	Then she cooks dinner for everyone.	She plays with the children.	She fetches the children from school.
She drives to work.	Then it's time to go to work. She puts on her uniform.	Or she reads a book.	Or she writes letters.
She makes breakfast for everyone.	She comes home at about 6.30.	She works until 6.00 in the morning.	She starts work at 10.00 at night.
		Lucy goes to bed – at 8.00 in the morning.	Her husband takes the children to school.

20 Work activities

VERBS

build houses	catch criminals	cook meals	cut hair
deliver letters	design machines	do experiments	draw plans
drive a bus	fly planes	grow crops	help sick people
help sick people	make things	paint pictures	pull out teeth
put out fires	repair cars	sell things	sell things
study	teach children	type letters	write articles

21 Household tasks

WORDS

baking	cleaning	cooking	dusting
gardening	ironing	laying the table	making the beds
mending	polishing	shopping	sweeping
tidying up	vacuuming	washing	washing up

21 Household tasks

ROLE CARDS

Sue **YOU DON'T MIND** making the beds, cooking, baking, washing. **YOU DON'T LIKE** cleaning the windows, ironing, washing up,	*Tim* **YOU DON'T MIND** vacuuming, gardening, dusting, mending. **YOU DON'T LIKE** polishing, tidying up, laying the table, shopping.	*Alice* **YOU DON'T MIND** cleaning the windows, ironing, polishing, tidying up. **YOU DON'T LIKE** vacuuming, gardening, making the beds, cooking.	*Sam* **YOU DON'T MIND** laying the table, shopping, washing up, sweeping. **YOU DON'T LIKE** dusting, mending, baking, washing.

Elementary Vocabulary Games

Addison Wesley Longman © J Hadfield 1998

21 Household tasks

PICTURES

Elementary Vocabulary Games
Addison Wesley Longman © J Hadfield 1998

22 Hobbies

WORDS

camping	cards	chess	climbing
collecting stamps	computer games	cycling	dancing
fishing	gardening	gliding	knitting
music	painting	photography	pottery
reading	riding	sailing	sewing
walking	windsurfing	yoga	

22 Hobbies

22 Hobbies

EQUIPMENT

23 Sports

EQUIPMENT

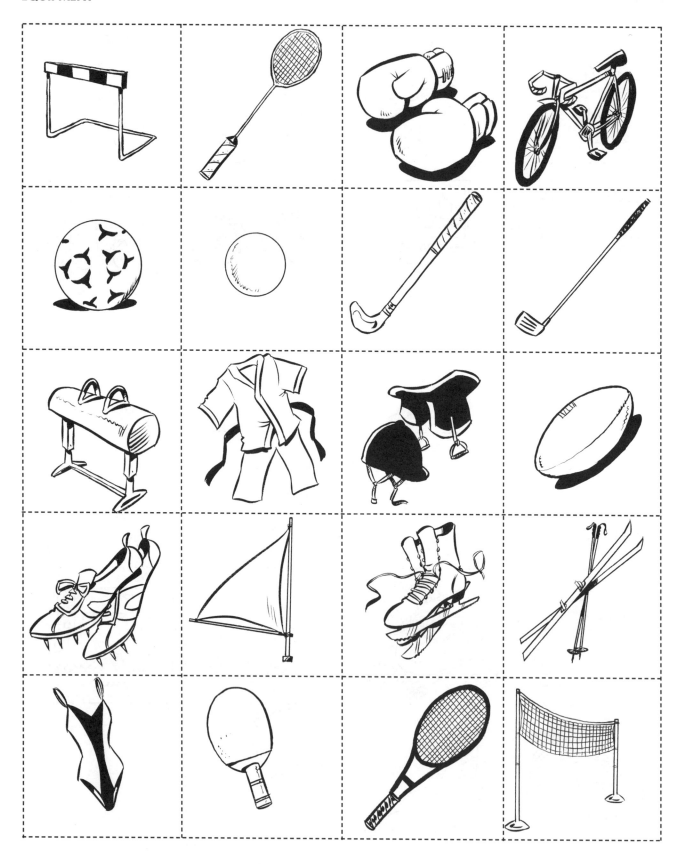

23 Sports

ACTIONS

97

23 Sports

WORDS

cycling	boxing	badminton	athletics
golf	hockey	handball	football
rugby	riding	judo	gymnastics
skiing	skating	sailing	running
volleyball	tennis	table tennis	swimming

24 Movements

PICTURES

24 Movements

WORDS

fall	crawl	climb	bend
lie	kneel	kick	jump
swim	stand	sit	run
carry	walk	turn	swing
hold	give	drop	catch
push	pull	pick up	lift
wave	touch	throw	take

24 Movements

Elementary Vocabulary Games
Addison Wesley Longman   © J Hadfield 1998

24 Movements

TABLEAUX

1 Beach

2 Station

25 Shapes and patterns

OBJECTS

102

25 Shapes and patterns

THE FLAG GAME

26 Materials

OBJECTS (2)

26 Materials

OBJECTS (1) pictures

26 Materials

OBJECTS (1) words

cotton	china	cardboard	bricks
metal	leather	gold	glass
rubber	plastic	paper	nylon
straw	stone	silver	silk
	wool	wood	wax

26 Materials

27 Town features

BUILDINGS (pictures)

Elementary Vocabulary Games
Addison Wesley Longman © J Hadfield 1998

27 Town features

BUILDINGS (words)

church	car park	café	bus station	bank
football ground	concert hall	cinema	temple	mosque
hospital	hotel	library	market	office block
pub	prison	post office	police station	park
skating rink	shopping centre	school	restaurant	railway station
	town hall	theatre	swimming pool	sports stadium

Elementary Vocabulary Games
Addison Wesley Longman   © J Hadfield 1998

27 Town features

ACTIVITIES

You get money here.	You can catch a bus here.	You can have a coffee here.	You can leave your car here.	You go here to pray.
You go here to pray.	You go here to pray.	You see films here.	You listen to music here.	You watch a match here.
You go here when you are sick.	You can sleep here.	You borrow books here.	You buy fruit and vegetables here.	You work here.
You can go for a walk here.	You go here when you are in trouble.	You post letters here.	Only criminals go here!	You can have a beer here.
You can catch trains here.	You can eat here.	You learn French here.	You can buy things here.	You go skating here.
You go running here.	You go swimming here.	You go to plays here.	You can get married here.	

27 Town features

DIRECTIONS

The railway station is at the end of the road, between the bank and the library.	The bank is at the end of the road on the left-hand side and opposite the library.	The library is at the end of the road, on the right-hand side and opposite the bank.	The post office is on the left-hand side, opposite the cinema and next to the bank.
The school is on the left-hand side, opposite the concert hall and next to the post office.	The theatre is on the left-hand side, next to the school and opposite the hotel.	The town hall is on the left-hand side, next to the theatre and opposite the shopping centre.	The restaurant is between the town hall and the church/mosque/temple on the left-hand side.
The church/mosque/temple is between the restaurant and the café on the left-hand side.	The café is the first building on the left, next to the church/mosque/temple.	The cinema is on the right, next to the library and opposite the post office.	The concert hall is between the cinema and the hotel on the right of the street.
The hotel is next to the concert hall, on the right and opposite the theatre.	The shopping centre is opposite the town hall and in front of the car park.	The pub is next to the shopping centre and opposite the restaurant.	The hospital is on the right, between the pub and the police station.
The police station is the first building on the right, in front of the football ground, next to the hospital opposite the café.	The swimming pool is behind the school and next to the skating rink.	The skating rink is next to the swimming pool and behind the theatre.	The bus station is behind the church/mosque/temple and next to the park.
The park is behind the café and next to the bus station.	The prison is behind the bank and on the left.	The sports stadium is on the right, behind the concert hall.	The office block is behind the cinema and next to the sports stadium.
The car park is on the right, behind the shopping centre.	The football ground is on the right, behind the police station.	The market is in the middle of the street.	

28 Street features

LABELS (words)

bus shelter	bus stop	crossroads	drain	kerb
lamp-post	letterbox	litterbin	pavement	road
telephone box	traffic island	traffic lights	zebra crossing	

28 Street features

STREET PICTURE 1

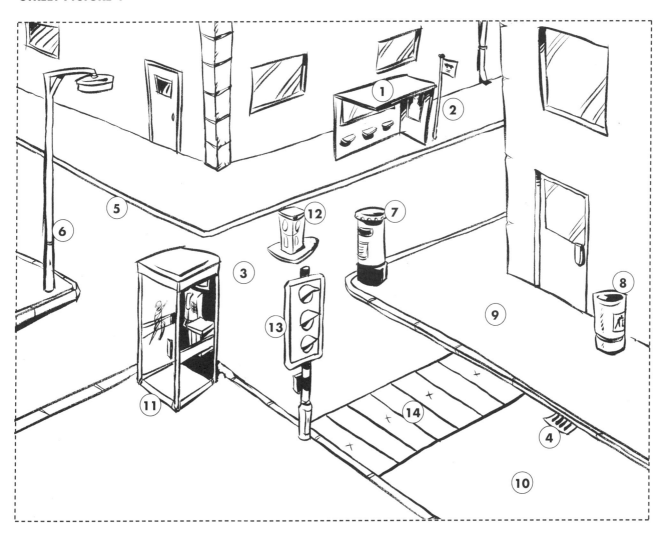

28 Street features

LABELS (numbers)

5	4	3	2	1
10	9	8	7	6
	14	13	12	11

28 Street features

STREET PICTURE 2

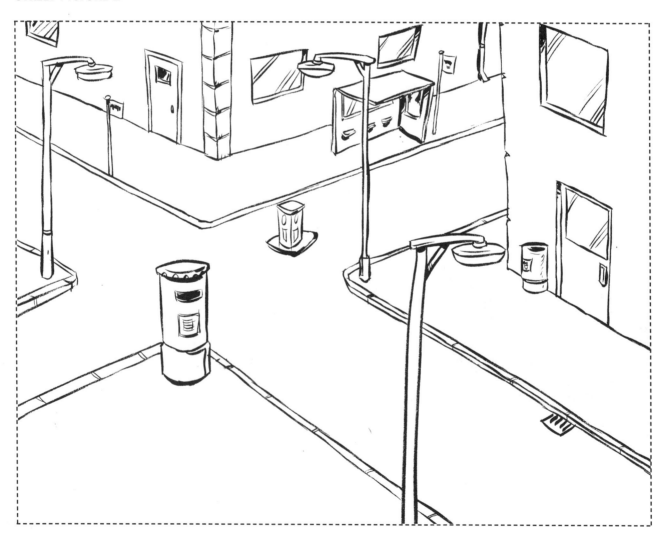

29 Places to live

HOUSES

29 Places to live

PEOPLE (1)

29 Places to live

PEOPLE (2)

30 The countryside

LANDSCAPE LABELS

beach	cliff	fence	field
forest	gate	hedge	hill
lake	marsh	mountain	path
pond	river	road	stream
valley	village	wood	

30 The countryside

SHEEP

30 The countryside

PICTURE

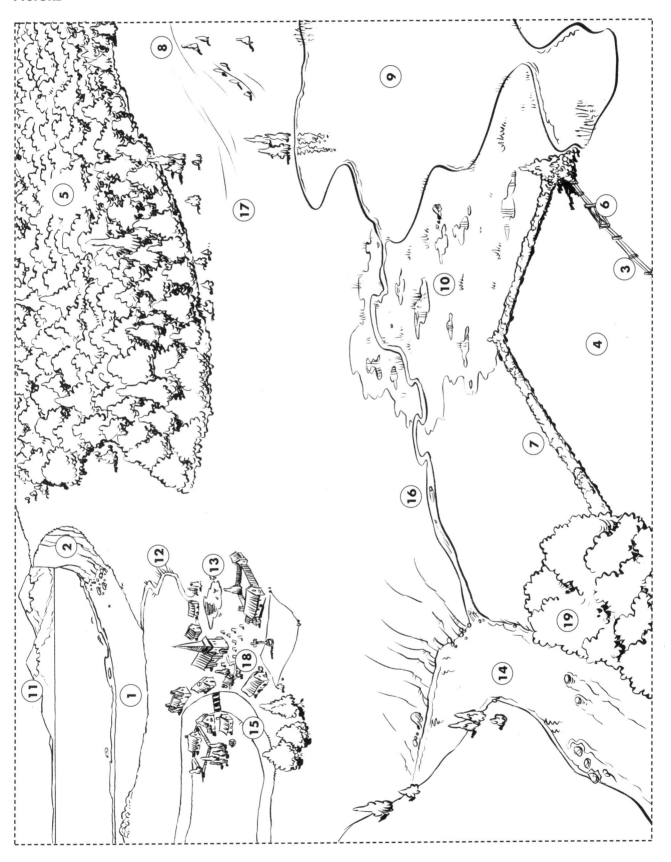

Rules sheets

5 THE ROBOT GAME
Rules
1. Play this game in groups of 3-4.
2. Shuffle the cards.
3. Deal out four cards to each player.
4. Put the rest of the cards face down in the middle.
5. Look at your cards. Are there any matching pairs? Put these down on the table in front of you.
6. Now begin. You must try to find matching pairs. Player 1 begins. Ask any other player if they have a card that matches one of your robots. **But do not show them your cards**. Ask, for example: 'Have you got a robot with a big round head, a square body and short arms?'
7. If the other player has the card, he must give it to Player 1.
8. If he does not have the card, Player 1 must take the top card from the pile.
9. Then it is the next player's turn.
10. At the end, the winner is the player with the most matching pairs.

11 THE HOUSEWORK GAME
Rules
1. Play this game in groups of 3-4.
2. You will have two sets of cards: task cards (with words) and object cards (with pictures).
3. Take one task card each.
4. Deal out four object cards to each player. Put the rest in a pile face down in the middle.
5. Look at your task card. Decide which objects you will need to do the task. You will need six objects. Your teacher will put a list on the board for you to choose from.
6. Now begin. You must try to collect the six objects you need.
7. Player 1 begins. Ask any other player if they have one of the objects you need, e.g. 'I need the teapot. Have you got it?'
8. If the player has the object, she must give it to Player 1. Then Player 1 can have another turn.
9. If not, then Player 1 must take a card from the pile in the middle.
10. Then it is the next player's turn.
11. The first player to get all the necessary items for the task is the winner.

13 FRUIT SALAD
Rules
1. Play this game in groups of 3-4.
2. Deal out five picture cards to each player.
3. Put the rest face down in a pile in the middle.
4. Look at your cards and sort them into **fruit** and **vegetables**.
5. You must try to collect five cards that are either all fruit or all vegetables. Decide which you are going to collect.
6. Player 1 begins. Ask any other player for a card that you need. If you are collecting fruit, you could ask, 'Have you got any cherries?' or 'Have you got a pineapple?', for example.
7. If the player has the card, he must give it to Player 1. Player 1 can take it and throw away a card she doesn't want. (Put it at the bottom of the pile.)
8. If he does not have the card, then Player 1 must take a card from the pile. If it is a card she wants, then she can keep it and throw another card away. If it is not a card she wants, then she can throw it away.
9. Then it is the next player's turn.
10. The winner is the first person to have five cards that are all fruit or all vegetables.

19 MAKE MY DAY
Rules
1. Play this game in groups of 3-4.
2. There are two packs of cards: action cards (with pictures) and time cards.
3. Deal out the time cards equally to everyone.
4. Put the action cards face down in the middle of the table.
5. Player 1 begins. Pick up an action card from the pile. Try to make a sentence about it, using one of the time cards in your hand, e.g. 'I eat breakfast at 7.00' or 'I go to work at 9.30'.
6. If the other players think your sentence could be true, e.g. 'I eat breakfast at 7.00', you can throw away your time card and the matching action card.
7. But if they think it isn't true, e.g. 'I eat breakfast at 3.30', then you must keep the time card in your hand and put the action card at the bottom of the pile (unless you have a good story to convince them it is true!).
8. Then it is the next player's turn.
9. The player who gets rid of all her cards first is the winner.

Rules sheets

20 JOBQUIZ
Rules
1. Play this game in groups of 3-4.
2. You will have two sets of job pictures.
3. One student is the Quizmaster. She should take one set of pictures and put them face down in front of her.
4. The others should deal out the other set of pictures equally between them. They can pick these up and look at them.
5. The Quizmaster picks up the first picture from her pile and looks at it. She must ask a *Who* question, e.g. 'Who flies a plane?' (looking at a picture of a pilot).
6. The player with the matching picture in his hand must answer, 'A pilot'. If he is right, he can throw away his card.
7. The player who gets rid of all his cards first is the winner.

21 DIVISION OF LABOUR
Rules
1. Play this game in groups of 3-4.
2. You will have a set of role cards and a set of picture cards.
3. Take a role card each. You all belong to the same family. The role card shows you who you are. Your mother has decided the house is dirty and needs cleaning. She has given you some jobs to do.
4. Now deal out the picture cards equally. Look at them. These are the jobs your mother has told you to do.
5. Compare them with the jobs listed on your role card. Which jobs don't you mind? Which jobs don't you like? Divide your pictures into two groups. Put the pictures of the jobs you don't mind on the table beside you.
6. In your hand you now have only pictures of jobs you don't like doing. The game is to give these to one of your 'brothers' or 'sisters', and to get them to give you jobs you prefer.
7. You can do this by making a bargain and exchanging cards, e.g. 'You do the dusting, I'll do the washing up' or 'You sweep the floors, I'll tidy up'.
8. The game ends when you all have the jobs you want. (If there are only three students in your group, there will be four jobs that no one wants to do! The winner will be the player who has none, or fewest of these.)

25 THE FLAG GAME
Rules
1. Play this game in groups of 3-4.
2. Shuffle the cards and deal out six to each player.
3. Put the rest face down in a pile.
4. In this game, you must collect matching flags. Look at your cards. Have you got any flags that match? If you have, take them out and lay them face down on the table beside you.
5. Player 1 begins. Ask any other player for a flag that matches one in your hand, e.g. 'Have you got a flag with a diamond inside a circle?'
6. If that player has the card, she must give it to Player 1 who can lay down the two matching cards together on the table.
7. If not, Player 1 must take another card from the pile.
8. Then it is the next player's turn.
9. The player who gets rid of their cards first is the winner.